D1084699

DIALOGUE WITH

R.D.
LAING

DIALOGUES IN CONTEMPORARY PSYCHOLOGY SERIES

Richard I. Evans, Series Editor

DIALOGUE WITH **GORDON ALLPORT**
DIALOGUE WITH **ERIK ERIKSON**
DIALOGUE WITH **ERICH FROMM**
DIALOGUE WITH **C.G. JUNG**
DIALOGUE WITH **R.D. LAING**
DIALOGUE WITH **JEAN PIAGET**
DIALOGUE WITH **CARL ROGERS**
DIALOGUE WITH **B.F. SKINNER**
PSYCHOLOGY AND **ARTHUR MILLER**

DIALOGUE WITH

R.D. LAING

Richard I. Evans

PRAEGER

PRAEGER SPECIAL STUDIES • PRAEGER SCIENTIFIC

Library of Congress Cataloging in Publication Data

Evans, Richard Isadore, 1922-
    Dialogue with R. D. Laing.

    (Dialogues in contemporary psychology series)
    Reprint. Originally published: R. D. Laing, the
man and his ideas. New York : Dutton, 1976. With a
new introd.
    Bibliography: p.
    Includes index.
    1. Laing, R. D. (Ronald David, 1927-
2. Psychiatrists—United States—Biography.
3. Psychiatry. 4. Clinical psychology. I. Laing, R. D.
(Ronald David), 1927-   . II. Title. III. Series:
Evans Richard Isadore, 1922-   . Dialogues with
notable contributors to personality theory.
RC339.52.L34E9 1981   616.89'0092'4 [B]   81-15372
ISBN 0-03-059928-8   AACR2

Published in 1981 by Praeger Publishers
CBS Educational and Professional Publishing
a Division of CBS Inc.
521 Fifth Avenue, New York, New York 10175 U.S.A.

© 1976 by Richard I. Evans and
   1981 by Praeger Publishers

123456789 145 987654321
Printed in the United States of America

To
my lovely wife
and children

Introduction to the Praeger Edition

In the few years that have passed since the first edition of **DIA-LOGUE WITH R. D. LAING** the field of psychiatry appears to have undergone an even greater degree of self-examination. Still to be resolved are the problems of evaluating various approaches to psycho-therapy, the use of drugs, newer understandings of brain mechanisms in mental disorders, hospitalization, and who the psychotherapist should be. Thus R. D. Laing's skepticism concerning psychiatry's ability to cope with such issues as presented in this volume, may be even more provocative. It is clear from his responses in our dialogue that Dr. Laing has evolved from reinforcing the perceptions of himself as a cult figure to a sophisticated observer of the mental health scene, who should be taken seriously. His views of the schizophrenic, for example, have contributed to a less rigid conception of such psycho-pathology. His experimentation with exotic techniques such as medita-tion may have contributed to current legitimization of such techniques even within the framework of behavior therapy. In short, many of R. D. Laing's speculative conceptions have been absorbed and inte-grated into contemporary clinical psychology and psychiatry. It is unfortunate that his reputation as a cult figure may have dissuaded many psychologists and psychiatrists from reading his publications. The present edition will afford an opportunity for an introduction to Dr. Laing's ideas at a time when perceptions of him are shifting.

ACKNOWLEDGMENTS

In the long process involved in filming and taping the dialogues with R. D. Laing, and transcribing, editing, and integrating them into the present volume, I am indebted to a great many individuals. Although space prohibits mentioning everyone who so kindly assisted me in this venture, I wish to express my appreciation to at least some of them.

Grateful acknowledgment is made to the University of Houston for permission to utilize the printed texts of the filmed and taped dialogue. Robert Cozens of the University of Houston functioned in the demanding role of technical director for the taping and filming sessions, and was of great help to me. Thanks also to Bette Keating for transcribing the original tapes of my discussion with Dr. Laing.

I am grateful for the support of the National Science Foundation, without which this project could not have been implemented.

Thanks are accorded to Peter Mezan for his provocative essay "R. D. Laing: Portrait of a Twentieth-Century Skeptic."

We appreciate Dr. Laing's willingness to allow us to reproduce one of his previously unpublished papers as an appendix to the present volume.

Special thanks are accorded psychology graduate student Bettye Earle Raines, who contributed to the editing, checked relevant bibliographical sources, and collated and typed the final manuscript.

We are most appreciative of the thoughtful assistance offered by John Reilly, Dr. Laing's assistant, throughout the work on this volume, and particularly for his outstanding job of incorporating Dr. Laing's reactions into the final form of the manuscript.

Finally, the wonderful cooperation of Ronald Laing cannot be emphasized enough. Not only was he willing to participate in the filming and audio-taping sessions involved in this project, discuss the format of this volume at a subsequent meeting in London, and make a number of excellent suggestions regarding the final form of the manuscript, but his genuine kindness, good humor, and stimulating insights contributed greatly to making this project a pleasant, as well as an exciting, experience.

RICHARD I. EVANS
Professor of Psychology
University of Houston

CONTENTS

INTRODUCTION

PART A: *Perspective on the Dialogue Style and Content*

This volume constitutes the tenth in a series based on dialogues with some of the world's outstanding contributors to psychology. To avoid possible misunderstanding about the goals of the dialogue style used in this volume, some perspective may be of value. Designed hopefully as an innovative teaching device, the series was launched in 1957, with completion of dialogues with the late Carl Jung and Ernest Jones, supported by a grant from the Fund for the Advancement of Education. The series is being continued under a current grant from the National Science Foundation. A basic purpose of the project is to produce, for teaching purposes, a series of films that introduce the viewer to creative contributors to the field of psychology and human behavior. We hope that these films may also serve as documents of increasing value to the history of the behavioral sciences.*

* The films are distributed by Macmillan Films, Inc., 34 MacQuesten Parkway S., Mt. Vernon, New York 10550.

The books in this series are based on edited transcripts of the dialogue, including audiotaped discussions as well as the contents of the films. These dialogues are designed to introduce the reader to the contributor's major ideas and points of view, conveying through the extemporaneousness of the dialogue style a feeling for the personality of the contributor.

When we completed the first book in the series based on dialogues with Jung and Jones (Evans, 1964), we thought the word *conversation* could best be used in the title to describe the process and content. We soon discovered that this implied to potential readers something a bit more casual and superficial than we had intended. Even though we emphasize spontaneity in the dialogues with our participants, this should not detract from the significance of the content. We would hope that a relatively informal discussion with an outstanding contributor to a discipline, as he seriously examines his own work, will not be less significant by virtue of its informality than more formal presentations. A more detailed description of the philosophy and techniques of this project is reported elsewhere (Evans, 1969c). However, a few points bearing on the content of these volumes can be emphasized here. Since the questions are intended to reflect many of the published writings of the interviewee, it might be expected that a comprehensive summary of this work is evoked. The selectivity necessary in developing the questions within a limited time interval does not always provide the basis for such an inclusive summary. Even so, as opposed to the increasing tendency to rely on secondary sources for information concerning our major contributors in the various disciplines, the material—films and books— resulting from our dialogues provides a novel "primary source" exposure to the ideas of outstanding persons. This, in turn, may stimulate the viewer or reader to go back to the original writings, which develop more fully the ideas presented through our *dialogue*.

The term *dialogue* was finally adopted instead of *conversation,* implying a more programmed content. *Dialogue,* however, also implies a challenge or confrontation with the individual being interviewed. To some, the term suggests that the questioner is using the individual being questioned as a tool to project the questioner's teaching role in the situation. My goals here would preclude either of these interpretations. It is my intention that these dialogues reflect a constructive, novel method of teaching, with my role as interviewer being neither the center of focus nor the critical challenger. The purpose of this book will be realized if I am perceived as providing a medium through which our distinguished interviewees can express their views. It is within the spirit of these teaching aims that our contributors so generously participate.

As was the case with subjects of the earlier books in the series, Jung and Jones (Evans, 1964), Fromm (Evans, 1966), Erikson (Evans, 1969a), Skinner (Evans, 1968), Arthur Miller (Evans, 1969b), Allport[1] (Evans, 1971), Piaget (Evans, 1973), Rogers (Evans, 1975a), and Lorenz (Evans, 1975b), it is hoped that the dialogue presentation allows the reader to be introduced to, or to reexamine, some of R. D. Laing's ideas through a relatively extemporaneous interchange. It should be pointed out, however, that in his writings, as Laing expresses himself in his own unique style,

[1] *Gordon Allport: The Man and His Ideas* received the 1971 American Psychological Foundation Media Award in the Book category.

he has the opportunity to rewrite and polish until he deems the finished product satisfactory. In the spontaneity of our discussion he is called upon to develop his ideas extemporaneously. I hope that this element of spontaneity may present more of the "man behind the book" while losing none of the ideas central to his thought. Because preservation of this naturalness of communication is essential to the purposes of each volume in this series, few liberties have been taken with the basic content of Dr. Laing's responses to my questions, although some editorial license had to be exercised to shift effectively from oral to printed communication in the service of accuracy, readability, clarity, and grammatical construction. So the dialogue presented here duplicates, insofar as possible, the tenor of the exchange between Dr. Laing and myself as it actually took place. In spite of the editing, which was necessary, it was a pleasant surprise to review our hours of discussion and realize how few deletions and alterations were required. We hope that this dialogue makes available to the reader some reactions not readily obtainable from Laing's previous presentations or from the secondary sources on his work in the literature.

Rather than attempt to summarize all of the major concepts presented in the dialogue, as we did in some of the previous volumes in this series, I shall again take the liberty, as I did in the Fromm, Skinner, and Erikson volumes, of briefly presenting frameworks that I find valuable in teaching personality theory to students, hoping they may in turn be of value to the reader of this book in comprehending the backdrop against which we may look at contemporary contributors to psychology such as R. D. Laing. Since, when Laing came on the scene, personality and psychotherapy were dominated by the influence of psychoanalytic theory, the evolution of psychoanalysis from traditional Freud to the so-called neo-Freudians figures prominently in the Laing dialogue. In fact, Laing himself originally received psychoanalytic training.

There are three frameworks around which I believe current approaches to personality psychology can be analyzed to help to locate any theoretical position within the matrix of general personality theory. These frameworks are really descriptive approaches to the understanding of personality that develop theoretically from basic orientations focusing around unconscious-oriented biological determinism (Freud, 1953), social environment-oriented cultural determinism (Karen Horney, 1937, 1945; Alfred Adler, 1927) or experience-oriented self-determinism (B. F. Skinner, 1968).

At various points in the dialogue Dr. Laing was given an opportunity to deal directly or indirectly with the differences among the three positions represented by the biological, cultural, and self-deterministic points of view. He feels that he has not ignored these conceptualizations; however, to him, generic bases of behavior vis-à-vis biological, cultural, or self-determinism are less important than focusing on the synthesis of the self, individually, and as an actor in society, very much in keeping with other individuals in the so-called Third Force humanist self-deterministic group. He exhibits a sophistication in existential perspective that appears at times to represent his position as philosophical as well as psychological. He often appears to be functioning in the role of social critic. Like others in this series, such as Jung, Fromm, and Rogers, it is difficult to see him as primarily a theorist or a practitioner in psychiatry or psychology. Perhaps more than any of the others, he seems to be anxious to serve as a catalyst—to make us a bit less certain about *any-thing* we believe.

In recent years, psychiatrists and psychologists have come to recognize the need to involve themselves with issues of immediate concern to society. The efforts of R. D. Laing appear to provide provocative base lines for such endeavors.

If the reader is encouraged to pursue the work of R. D. Laing in greater depth, a relatively complete bibliography of his writings is provided in the reference section of this book.

Personal Impressions: A New Look at a Controversial Psychiatrist

In the process of filming and audio-taping several hours of dialogue with R. D. Laing and in a subsequent meeting with him, I had occasion to observe and to interact closely with this man who appears to be the center of so much controversy. Very much on my mind as I approached the first interview session were the articles I had read that described him as "difficult to deal with," "unfair and demanding," "obstreperous," "discourteous and ridiculing." In fact, several psycho-analysts I know had described him as quite "schizy" although few had actually met him. One psychiatrist, who recalled meeting Laing in 1967, described that year as a troubled period in Laing's life, one that might have accounted for some of these lingering percep-tions. Also, I think Laing's "role-playing" style and subtle humor are occasionally misunderstood.

During the film and taping sessions, and more re-cently, when we met in London to discuss final work on this project, I found him to be charming and cooperative. He manifested none of the aberrant behavior attributed to him. We met for dinner during this most recent visit, and as we explored some of his many interests—music (he is an accomplished pianist), poetry, the theatre, the current political situation—I was impressed with both his depth and his perspicacity. He seemed pleased with the early chapters of this book that had been forwarded to him, and I was truly flattered when he sought my reaction to his newest publication, *Why Did the Peacock Scream?* (in press). As I read it, he awaited my reaction with unconcealed anticipation, and appeared to be delighted when I told him that I felt the significance of this work seemed to go far beyond psychiatry and, indeed, in its approach, suggested a poetic form much like the work of Dylan Thomas. This work will obviously be considered from an existential perspective, even as *Knots* (Laing, 1970b) was, but most of all, I found his droll style of writing quite disarming.

One of his major concerns at that time seemed to be an old house that he and his wife, Jutta, had just bought and were in the process of refurbishing. We talked about the problems inherent in dealing with contractors and keeping within a budget—certainly very ordinary problems that most of us can appreciate.

I was impressed by a certain humility that Laing displays, rarely taking credit for the ideas he employs in his work and, in fact, trying very hard to credit those individuals he thinks were really responsible for the ideas, both in his own work and in the work of others. For example, he freely credited Harry Stack Sullivan (1953) for some ideas concerning interpersonal transactions that had been ascribed to him. As we discussed Jung's (Evans, in press) archetypes, he hastened to note that this concept did not actually orig-

inate with Jung. He has a great sense of scholarly and
historical perspective, and a wide knowledge of the
philosophical, sociological, and psychological literature, as well as the psychiatric. There is an openness
about his views and his assessment of himself that is
truly refreshing. "One of the ways I'm different from
the other people that you've had in your series," he
told me, "is that they have already made their significant contributions, and I feel that my major contributions are yet to come."

A widespread current belief is that even though
Laing was trained as a psychoanalyst, he condemns
psychoanalysis completely. Actually, he seems to think
that Freudian theory continues to have value. In my
informal conversations with him he simply did not
come across in the dogmatic manner often attributed
to him. For example, he doesn't really say that there is
no identifiable syndrome that can be labeled schizophrenia, or that so-called schizophrenic states may be
problem-resolution processes. He doesn't suggest that
all schizophrenics be left alone, eventually to resolve
their disorder, but he does say that he finds it interesting that we have not left schizophrenics alone enough
really to study the entire course of the disease, and
that we should at least explore the cause of this disorder.

I got the impression that he enjoys making extreme
statements for their effect as a catalytic device, part of
his admitted role as a skeptic in the old philosophical
tradition, and that he makes such statements with a
realistic understanding of the functions of the traditional beliefs that may need to be shaken by extreme
statements. In his own efforts, however, such as the
"Kingsley Hall" type of community treatment centers,
he absolutely refrains from any unqualified claims for

their success, and prefers to discuss them as experimental efforts with certain reported and inferred results. There is about him a great sense of the experimental, and a flexibility that enables him to view his own efforts, and those of others, in a critical but creative manner. For example, whereas he was much taken with Gregory Bateson's (1956) double-bind theory (e.g., the idea that the child is torn by conflicting input from the parents) in his early work, and particularly with its specific applications to family situations in the etiology of psychopathology, he now says that his research makes him wonder whether his concept may not be too general for Bateson's more precise meaning.

He seems to be a shy person, and he confesses to a problem in oral communication, tending to digress from a line of thought, although this characteristic did not appear in our casual face-to-face encounters and was rarely evident in the more formal discussions on which this book is based.

Developing a really deep relationship with him over a period of time might be somewhat difficult, but in my limited contact with him I found him to be warm, open, and friendly. There was nothing in his behavior at any point that supported the image of him as being rather hostile or difficult, if not deeply disturbed. How he might have acted earlier in his career, under different conditions, perhaps under harassment by the media for his alleged "catering to the drug culture," is another matter. I can only report that R. D. Laing struck me as a clever, imaginative, thoughtful man, capable of rare intellectual brilliance and great compassion, whose communication patterns unfortunately cloud this image.

PART B: R. D. Laing: Portrait of a Twentieth-Century Skeptic
BY PETER MEZAN*

In the mind's eye, under the magical sign of the caduceus, stands a gaunt, pixielike man in the garb of a prophet—acid at his right hand, revolution at his left, his head haloed with the clear light of an Oriental paradise, his eyes intimating madness—crushing beneath his avenging foot the serpent of the Western rationalist tradition.

Sprung upon an unwittingly ready world in 1960, with the publication of a lucid, deceptively innocent book called *The Divided Self*, the name R. D. Laing sank into the minds of my generation like a crystal into a solution, precipitating a growth unaccountably huger and weirder than any of the events that begot it, and it is growing every day. All the time's most plaintive urges and most temperamental ideas cluster around the image of this elusive Scottish psychoanalyst as around the hero

* Mr. Mezan's forthcoming book on R. D. Laing will be published by Pantheon Books.

of a chivalric romance. Radicals honor him as a philosopher of revolution. Universities teach his books in courses of literature, psychology, and philosophy. Mental patients quote him reflexively at their psychiatrists, who often crimson reflexively at the mention of him. Runaways, street freaks, and disillusioned GIs pack his books in their shoulder bags as manuals for making sense of a berserk world, and intellectuals, who have taken Laing's ideas about sanity and madness as part of their conjectural furniture, totter between doubt and regard for a man whose ideas people seem to take as seriously as they do real life.

Fame like that must be either the distillation of a collective dream or, like a lot of fame, arrant nonsense and baloney. Yet, to explain how hundreds of thousands of allegedly reasoning people come to buy it, maintain it, and enhance it, one must suppose it to be intelligible nonsense, or at least irresistible baloney. For the fact of the matter is that a lot of people have a sense that this man has read and touched their most secret minds, and no one is more curious about it than R. D. Laing himself, who hadn't quite foreseen that so many people would be so interested.

"I get quite a lot of letters," Laing said recently to a group of psychoanalysts who wanted to know what he made of it all. "People tell me how they read *The Politics of Experience* (Laing, 1967) ten times and still carry it around with them. They say it completely changed their lives, that it made them see everything differently, that it was the first time they'd ever discovered someone else thinking the way they were thinking. I really don't know what to make of that. My mind must have been in synchrony with the EEG waves, or something, of an extensive array of people. And I got it into words that had a sort of rhythm and

incantatory tone, not just ordinary prose. At the end
of World War II, a lot of people seemed to feel something like that about the writings of Camus. Of course,
that says nothing at all about whether what I was saying was true or not. It just happened to coincide with
what a lot of people were feeling. Several people even
wrote to me saying that *they* had written *The Divided
Self!* (Laing, 1960). They wrote it! In other words, I'd
read the whole thing off their brains—we shared one
mind. They were quite friendly about it. No one accused me of stealing it. It didn't seem to make any difference. Of course, when I wrote it, I felt that very few
people were feeling the same way. But that was the
feeling everyone had—hundreds of thousands of people
all feeling the same way, namely, that no one else is
feeling that way. I seemed to put that realization into
circulation."

And what are these deep, sneaking feelings that so
many putatively normal, reasoning people have all
had, unknown sometimes to themselves as well as to
each other until Laing named them, made sense of
them, and gave them public credence? That we are all,
in our fashions, truly mad, schizoid, doubly divorced,
once from ourselves and once from virtually everyone
and everything else; that most of us, most of the time,
including most psychiatrists, are patently out of our
senses—literally, of sight, sound, taste, touch, smell,
and proprioception; that helplessly mixing up the present with swarms of memories, wishes, and fantasies,
until we no longer perceive anything either clearly or
truly, we yet persist in making inferences about the
world that are presumptuous past the point of delusion and act certain when really we are nearly blind;
that what we fondly appeal to as normality is a cruel
fiction based on no more or less than what most people

at a given time guess they, and the others, think is so—
a narrow majority agreement fraught with terrible contradictions about what shall and shall not be regarded
as real or sane or good, that we enforce out of fear of
too much uncertainty, and at the cost of appalling al-
ienation; and that what is ordinarily called madness—
going crazy—may actually be a process of coming ter-
rifyingly awake to just those "normal" contradictions
and confusions to which most of us are ordinarily fast
asleep.

These are some of the suspicions, usually shoved out
of the mind, that Laing's books abruptly awakened,
and that the world's perfectly evident insanity keeps
seeming to confirm. For is it perennial to our natures,
or some kind of a bluff, or are we the first generation
seriously to suspect (or fear or hope) that we are
crazy? Few people behave the way they feel, or feel
the way they think, or think the way they behave. At
first one imagines that one is mad, then that everyone
else is mad, then that we're all mad. We suppose we
need a doctor. And who should turn up but Dr. Ronald
David Laing; and the ticklish thought arises that here,
perhaps, may be a wise man who will make the rough
places plane and tell us how to live in the world. Either
that, or that he is crazy himself, since anyone who sees
what he seems to see must be either wise or crazy.

But that is only where Laing's fame begins. Beyond
that there is an endless confection of rumors and stories and guesses about him, some adoring, some anathe-
matizing. People have it on good authority that Laing
is an illuminated saint if not a Buddha incarnate, or a
foxy cracker-barrel charlatan, a pedantic, armchair,
bourgeois revisionist, a magus, a boob, an ascetic, a
voluptuary or, most likely of all, a dangerous, schizophrenic acid- (or coke or smack or speed or booze)

head, angling to seduce others into getting off on the same schizy number. Even those who've met him more than once disagree, sometimes from one day to the next, about whether he is by disposition freaky or serene, reckless or cautious, cold or compassionate, manipulative or permissive, arrogant or humble. The only thing about which everyone agrees is that however he appears to them is utterly convincing, devoid of sham, unquestionably his real self. And this makes for no small problem if, out of bewildered curiosity about the strange state of the mid-twentieth-century mind, one wants to discover just who this incomparably fabled man is, and what it is about him that, apparently without his connivance, triggers among such multitudes almost any fantasy you may like to pick from the contemporary fantasy spectrum.

I have other motives too—a chronic fascination with unusual selves and (not always the same thing) with people who, for no obvious reasons at all, scare me. Laing fits both bills. From all the stories about him, one might conclude either that he has no self, or that he doesn't know himself what it is, or that, being any self and all selves, he juggles and manipulates them like a master puppeteer (or actor, or psychopath), all of which may amount to the same thing and any of which may well strike you as a bit spooky. For even conceding stalemate over the riddle of what is and is not real, I confess I do expect a certain constancy of the external world. At least I tend to hope that someone I meet one day will resemble himself sufficiently the next, psychologically as well as physically, that I will recognize him, and that if you met him too, we'd agree we had met the same person. In Laing's case, it is not always so certain. In fact, even though in the several years I have known him I have yet to see anything

about him so freaky or untoward as to seriously upset my applecart, still I confess I am more than ever
prepared to accept that almost anything anybody
thinks about him may be as true as not true. Moreover,
I cannot rid myself of the feeling that there's something he is either doing or not doing that is an essential ingredient to all this, though it's very hard to tell
exactly what.

I don't mean to be mystical about this. Laing may
not be ordinary, but he isn't unrecognizable. Some
things about him—certain traits and mannerisms one
could probably trace to a lower-middle-class upbring-
ing in the slums of Glasgow—are fairly constant, such
as a rather dour unsociability and high seriousness
mixed with equally studious delinquency. But beyond
that, to put it plainly, Laing is a very moody man, in a
unique sense. Indeed, his repertory of moods is so vast
that he is always upsetting even the most benign expectations. Furthermore, whatever mood he is in he
seems astonishingly unafflicted by any degree of self-
consciousness. In a single evening I have seen him run
the gamut of human emotions, taking on one distinct
persona after another, even changing sex, and in each
one appearing to be wholly himself. This is quite a per-
formance. It can also, from a certain point of view,
appear to be quite mad. But there is another point of
view from which it can look inspired, as though
Laing's behavior, cultivated or not, tended effortlessly
to counterfeit that canny sort of madness subsumed in
the ancient sense, almost lost to us, that the folly of the
wise man and the wisdom of the fool are each other's
nearest counterparts.

"The contract I've made with my mind," Laing explains, "is that it is free to do anything it cares to do."

Now, frankly, there is nothing more extraordinary

under the sun than a human who can freely entertain whatever thoughts, memories, feelings, fantasies, dreams, or waking perceptions his mind may bring up, without immediately interfering in all manner of strange ways—by repressing, denying, splitting, reversing, projecting, taking these to be real and those to be unreal—striving automatically either to get rid of them because they're uncomfortable or to' hold onto them because they feel good. And it is in this sense that, if Laing seems mad, it may only be from the madder vantage point of normality. For the practical meaning of keeping such a contract is that his ideas—what he thinks—are as little removed from what he's feeling, or how he behaves, as he can manage—an integrity that, in my experience with intellectuals, is unique, and that, incidentally, is psychiatry's own criterion of sanity. And one of Laing's ideas is that there is no such thing as a *self*—that for all he's tried, he has been unable to persuade himself either philosophically or by experience that there is such a thing, or that his particular repertory of feelings, thoughts, and sensations, which is what most people seem to mean by a self, is any more substantial, or true, or real than those of the craziest people he's met or treated. And nothing, surely, is more likely to quicken people's spookiest fantasies than a man who appears happily to have no identifiable self, or only the loosest and most mercurial of commitments to what one might take to be a self.

That, anyhow, was the best theory I had when I was invited along for part of his coast-to-coast tour of America—fifteen public lectures in as many cities—and I decided to test my theory as I watched him meet the people who think whatever it is they think about him.

Early on a wet, smoky November morning in London, two days before his departure, Laing stood barefoot in the perpetual night of his study, his head slung between hunched shoulders, his whole frame a little cocked, like a hobgoblin about to crouch. Indeed, there was something distinctly elfin about his whole appearance: a small, economical body with large, knobby bones, capricious hazel eyes that were always taking one unawares, an impressively large nose, and a face craggy with slopes and furrows, which seemed to decompose and compose into more ages and expressions, all looking to be equally in repose, than any face I'd ever seen.

"What are you going to say in America, Ronnie?"

"I really have no idea at all."

He didn't seem perturbed about it. Indeed, since last spring, when he and his wife, Jutta, and their two small children had returned from India and Ceylon, where he had spent a year resting and studying meditation, very little seemed to perturb him. Before then, since the last days of Kingsley Hall—Laing's famous community experiment where therapists and psychotics lived together on equally impromptu terms and which had broken up in 1970—he'd been getting increasingly morose and withdrawn, showing little interest in anything, refusing all requests for interviews, keeping to himself. Now it was different. His friends, remarking on how well he looked and how open he'd become, said he had won equanimity. He said he had finally managed to get free of his passionate and habitual attachment to the intellect. He still remained largely solitary—seeing few patients, reading, practicing yoga, playing the clavichord until all hours—but he was agreeable and accessible to anyone seeking him out. The American tour was dramatic evidence of that. The first time he went to New York, he flew out again two hours later, having decided that was an environment he was just not at all ready to enter.

"You know the airport scene in *A Hard Day's Night,* when the fans tear the Beatles' clothes off? Well, that's what people are expecting you may be in for, that sort of thing. I got a letter."

Laing's eyes lit up.

"It'll certainly be interesting. I mean, not many people have the chance to experience things from a position like that."

The thought amused him. He considered it for a moment, staring sightlessly over my shoulder and massaging his gums with a toothpick. Then he grinned.

"The point is, I'm about to become more famous than I've ever been before, and in a completely different way. A poster—that kind of famous. Someone told me he'd seen one already in New York. Up to now, I suppose I've been famous mostly to people in psychology or psychiatry or people who generally consort with ideas. Funny that it should be happening now when it means the least to me."

Again he fell silent; then: "I mean, no one like *me*, to my knowledge, has ever been famous that way before. Not in their lifetime, anyway. Most posters are of a different kind of thing, like Marilyn Monroe or Bogart. I don't know exactly what a poster of me would be representing. The Che Guevara thing wasn't the same, and I don't think Timothy Leary ever made it to that."

He looked at me quizzically, smiling with the caprice of a boy contemplating a prank.

"Becoming this kind of famous opens up whole new dimensions!" he laughed, his hand making a flourish in the air and then dropping limp at his side. "I don't know what that'll be like, but it will certainly be interesting."

In New York, Suite 608 at the Algonquin Hotel, at the moment, was field headquarters to assorted mem-

bers of the R. D. Laing Bandwagon. Peter Robinson, a
tall man with a gaunt, kindly look reminiscent of Abe
Lincoln, who'd directed the film, *Asylum*, a study of a
Laingian community in London, and who would be
making a film of this tour if enough money came
through to make a print, was expostulating furiously
at his cameraman, Dick Adams, who was ignoring him
to help Bill, the sound man, set up and test the lights.
Laing, over the years, had cultivated an indifference
to being filmed—he said he hardly noticed it—though he
always gave everyone in range the option to refuse it
if the camera made them nervous. It was just as well,
because for the next thirty-three days everything he did,
everywhere he went, every public moment and any
private ones that could be wangled, Robinson and his
crew and the magic eye would be there to catch it.
So would Danny Halperin—ex-Paris-based reporter, ex-
jazz critic, ex-design consultant, ex-rock promoter, ex-
junkie, and old friend of Laing's—who had contrived
to come along on the tour as his factotum. Danny was
always either on the phone or on his feet, and usually
in a jitter. Today he was all three, and also waving for
an appointments schedule from Elaine Sperber from
New Line Cinema, the outfit that (for a third of the
take) was organizing the whole operation. This was
New Line's second venture in the lecture-tour business.
The first had featured Norman Mailer, who'd returned
utterly exhausted. It was run by Bob Shaye, a good-
humored, explosively ambitious young man who had
just walked in the door and started arguing with
Danny and Peter about who had arranged what with
whom, and by what rights, concerning the filming and
taping of the tour. Laing lay sprawled and barefoot at
one end of the sofa, grinning with enjoyment at another affray underway between Elaine Sperber and

Lynn Jacobs, in charge of publicity for Pantheon Books, Laing's publishers, about what priorities to give which magazines, newspapers, TV and radio shows, none of which Laing had ever read, seen, or heard.

Also, beyond a certain boyish relish he sometimes took in the prospect of a Laing Bandwagon steaming across Europe and the Americas, altering the shape of the Western mind, he didn't seem too interested. He hadn't asked for any of this retinue, and he certainly had no interest in the mechanics of it.

Some of the Bandwagon found this slightly exasperating. For without doing or saying anything in particular, Laing had a way of making one feel distinctly superfluous and, moreover, neurotic to be exasperated about it. Part of it could be attributed to the mystique, which was of such peculiar force that it almost always induced instant awe and anxiety. But there was also something about his presence, a degree of impassivity and self-containment, that affected even strangers in much the same unsettling way it did his acquaintances and which was extremely difficult to adjust to. He seemed to make a virtue of Glaswegian bad manners, for although he was scrupulously considerate in his own fashion, his only criterion for behavior was that people be decent and honest, which, for him, was subtle and far-reaching, and did not usually include small talk or giving approval or showing that he liked you, or any of the formulaic interactions that most of us depend on for our social ease. Nor, apparently, did it include much interest in questions of promotional strategy. The upshot was that nobody quite knew what to expect of him, what he had in mind, or what would interest him. Generally, he showed little more than a benign indifference to suggestions, a response—or lack of it—that neither encouraged nor discouraged and that betrayed no special inclinations to latch onto. Or, if he did take an interest, it was usually from some strange, tentative angle of his own that would as likely disappear as unpredictably as it arose.

To the promoters, who were accustomed to stars having marked earthly preferences and desires, this Olympian viewpoint was quite a novelty. It was all very well being illuminated and unattached and equanimous and all, yet here was this whole promotional apparatus all keyed up and humming and ready to zap an ailing, anorexic America, which ate up and vomited culture heroes like candy, only to be left still famished and crazy, with the one man, the unique phenomenon, who had been awaited for over a decade, in whom the wisdom of the East and the science of the West had met—wake up, sick people, the doctor's here!!

Only the doctor, smiling curiously from the sofa in Suite 608, wasn't playing along.

"Ronnie, you're being no help at all," moaned Lynn Jacobs. "The lineup for interviews is already a mile long, and we got requests this morning from *Penthouse* and *Reader's Digest*. And they've asked to see you for the Op Ed page of the *Times*. And by the way, we accepted the "Today Show" for Monday. And *The Voice* wants to interview you, but you're having lunch that day with . . . I don't see how . . ."

"What's the difference?" Laing asked good-naturedly, picking his way across the lighting cables to a big basket of fruit. "Where do you draw the line? If one's going to go in for this sort of thing at all, one might as well go the whole way. Anyway, it's possible that no matter what you say or to whom, the overriding effect of the medium itself can't be overcome. It's a problem of context. You have to decide that before you can decide about anything else."

He turned to her, smiling, munching on an apple.

"I'll leave it up to you. You know more about it than I do."

When it came to discussing the first public talk at Hunter College, however, Laing was suddenly more interested. In the past he had generally avoided these huge, lopsided formats. He either wouldn't, or couldn't, give a formal lecture into a void. Talking to people was a matter of responding to minute physical signs in proximity, and without such cues to give him a sense of where his audience stood or what they wanted, he tended to ramble and pursue thoughts almost by free association. To a big crowd this was not always as interesting as it might sound. It would be an experiment, then, though as yet he had no idea what kind. But it was in some measure under his control since it involved choices about how to deploy himself. He thought he'd get an Oriental rug and just come out on stage and sit on it. He wasn't certain yet, but probably he'd wear a blue Oxford shirt, a brown cashmere sweater, brown trousers, and shoes and socks. Lynn Jacobs thought he was kidding.

"For God's sake, Ronnie, you're not an entertainer!"

"I am!" Laing spun around, waving the apple. "I don't see how else to regard this than as show business. Besides, all these things—what to wear, whether to stand up or sit down, behind a table or on a table, shoes or no shoes—they're all decisions, and they might as well be conscious. They are just as important a part of the statement as anything else, fraught with fantasies and all kinds of symbolic value. If I wore a dark suit and tie, it would be a completely different thing. But that's not where I'm at."

Where he was usually "at" during most of the week in New York was on the sofa in Suite 608, barefoot, wearing brown velvet trousers and a maroon velour shirt, while outside over the wash of the rain, sound trucks blared slogans and the windows shook with the screaming of the engines from the fire station down the street.

Inside, on one such afternoon, the camera was turning, the soundman was crouched on the floor, three mikes were on the coffee table, two photographers were creeping up on the sofa from either side, a reporter was waiting his turn in one of the chairs, and a girl from *Newsweek* was saying, "This is going to be very superficial, because I don't know anything about your work. I work for a section of the magazine called Newsmakers, and all we'd like, really, is something witty or shocking, so maybe you could just say what you expect to be doing in America."

"I expect to be spending most of my time in this or that hotel room, alone, doing nothing."

That was one way of putting it. Having arrived in New York with nothing in particular in mind to say, and no notion of what might happen, Laing simply hung out like a tourist visiting the landscape of his own phenomenal reputation, quite prepared to talk to anybody who wanted to talk to him about whatever was on their minds. That meant, of course, that they had to know what was on their minds, which was not always, or even mostly, the case. Quite often Laing would simply not respond to anything less. He was not uncordial about it. Compared to the usual, he went out of his way to be sociable, but he could sometimes just sit there, impassive, showing neither expectation nor disappointment, until the gap between what people said and how they looked had disappeared. To many people, including a number of experienced reporters, this was more than they had bargained for. Stripped of the formal comforts and anonymity of the usual interview situation, they found themselves plunged into something far more demanding and immediate, eye to eye with a man who spoke only to them, and gave them all his attention. No retreat behind an impersonal question, no recourse to theory or a placatory show of erudition escaped him. As though the mystique weren't enough to cope with, you had to *converse*, for God's sake. The result was sometimes naked panic.

"Why does Ronnie make people so nervous, so uptight?," his wife asked. "I felt tremendously relieved when I first met him. He was so open, so relaxed, there was so little shit about him, so few numbers."

"Maybe that's it," I said. "People aren't used to that. We tend to identify each other by our numbers. The common mark of our humanity is our mutual embarrassment, our deceit, and our neuroses. With him, there isn't much to go on somehow. People can't tell where he is." Did I believe that? When I first met him he was relaxed all right, while I had the distinct sensation of being suddenly out on a limb by myself, cold and scared and quite transparent. It was nothing he was doing. He just wasn't helping. "Anyway," I added, "when you first met him, you didn't know who he was."

Norman Mailer knew, however. And even Mailer, in his way an equally signal and renegade moment of the contemporary Western mind with a considerable mystique and balls of his own, seemed uncharacteristically diffident and uncertain when he and Laing met in the dressing room to tape a TV show.

"I don't know what we're going to talk about, do you?," Mailer asked.

"No."

"But at least we're pretty sure not to bore each other. I really think we're a funny fit, in a way. Of course, if we get going and are any good, the audience isn't going to like it. It's a peculiar medium. People don't like it to be good. It keeps them up. They like it to be soporific, to prepare them for sleep."

"Mmm."

It was a chivalrous encounter. Laing was shy, professorial, stammering. Mailer was subdued and complimentary. They talked about *karma*, the transmigration of souls, the doctrine that our actions in one life affect the next.

"That may be the most powerful motivation we possess," Mailer said. "It's also the only hypothesis that explains anything. So long as we assume that when we die there is no hereafter, no eschatology, that we're neither rewarded nor punished, then I think we just run into one philosophical impasse after another. Human nature becomes absolutely impossible to describe in any way at all."

"It may be," Laing said. "The position I've found the most challenging is that, in fact, there's no entity whatever, even in this lifetime, and that the appearance of such is an illusion. There is no being, no person, no self. But there's the appearance of a pattern. The mind, which isn't an entity either, identifies itself with part of the phenomena that face it, and we take that to be ourselves. And so any discussion about when we begin or end—at birth, before birth, this time, last time, whether it's a hundred times or one time—is one of those illusory, quasi-magical fabrications, like a mirage."

The moderator turned to Laing. "Does that really mean anything to you? How can you experience the nonexistence of your self?"

"For quite sustained periods of time, I've had the

experience, which I simply report as another experience, that my experience of myself was an illusion."

"What did you think of it?" Mailer asked me later. "Tame."

"You wanted the two lions to tear into each other? I tell you, I was feeling very equivocal and uncertain about it. I wasn't sure what to say. Usually it's easy—you have one charged mind and one empty one, and its just a matter of pouring from one into the other. But this was two charged minds, and I had no idea what was going to happen."

Nobody ever did with Laing. Least of all Mrs. Elizabeth Fehr, the vivacious matriarch and spiritual midwife of a Manhattan group of some thirty persons—all of whom she regarded as her children in the sense that she had taken them each through ritual reenactments of their births, down a thirty-foot-long mattress, usually more than once—who turned up one morning. She had come to the right place. Laing was delighted. The tribulations of the birth experience, which he was now demonstrating on the floor, lying on his back with his hands and feet in the air, were a major preoccupation of his.

"Apart from the exigencies of life in the womb, and the horrors of the passage down the birth canal, just consider the quality of the first sights, sounds, tastes, touches, and smells the average newborn infant is subjected to in a modern Western hospital delivery room. Virtually the first thing that happens is the clamping and cutting of the cord, immediately inducing umbilical shock with the sudden blockage of the circulation, instead of simply waiting for the cord to close off by itself, and for the infant's breathing to take over naturally, of its own accord. I mean, physiologically, every red emergency light in the body must start flashing and signaling a critical threat to life, that suddenly, out of nowhere, one's life is in danger and unless one does something fast, within a few seconds, one is going to die. It's almost guaranteed that for the rest of one's life, there's going to be a terrible fear associated with that whole area of the body, the umbilicus and the genitals."

He doubled up on the floor, demonstrating the convulsive jerk that an infant's body makes when the cord is cut.

"And it's so unnecessary. That's why I don't like to call it 'birth trauma,' just birth experience. Because we just don't know how much of it is necessary. I'm sure a lot of it isn't. They say the nervous tracks for registering such things aren't developed yet, are not yet myelinated, so the infant can't really experience it. But you can actually see it. You can *see* it!"

He climbed back up onto the sofa and described to Mrs. Fehr his history of respiratory ailments, culminating in asthma, which he demonstrated with bulging eyeballs and much frightening wheezing, and how he had come to locate its origins in some part of his own birth experience, and so had all but managed to free himself of it.

"Birth is the heaviest experience of our lives. I really don't see why people are so reluctant to see that. According to the Buddha, birth is one of the nine forms of human suffering. And Freud knew about it. And Otto Rank and the Reichians. Even Janov—that's what he is on about. He may be rather crudely oversimplified about it. It's not the whole picture, one does have experiences after birth. But in another sense, we're dying and being reborn every minute, so how it went the first time is quite likely to be mapped onto all our subsequent experience."

Mrs. Fehr, already late for a meeting with some leading astrologers, reluctantly stood up to go.

"For years I've wanted to meet you. You think the way I do. You know, some people think I'm crazy."

"Well, a lot of people think I'm crazy, too," Laing smiled.

At the door she asked for the time and place of his birth.

"October 7, 1927, at 5:15 P.M. in Glasgow."

The procession through Suite 608 was relentless. People came and went; I contemplated my theory; and Laing still searched for signs of what all these people wanted from him, and grew steadily more bored in the process. Hour after hour, the same questions about what's mad and what's sane, the same misconceptions, that inexplicable fear, and a few instances of overt hostility. Margaret Mead, the anthropologist, refused to speak on the same radio show with a man who'd left a wife and five children, none of whom she'd ever met. The elevator man at the Algonquin went berserk and screamed at Laing for leaning on the bell. Laing screamed back.

And there was Professor Amitai Etzioni. It was at an intimate soiree in a handsome Bank Street town house. Professor Etzioni, chairman of the sociology department at Columbia University, stood peering down the staircase with his plate full of food and, without realizing whom he was addressing, chortled derisively to Jutta Laing, "Suppose we go down and see just what this little Scotsman, this Dr. Charisma, has to say for himself."

The other guests had already arranged themselves

in a circle on the living-room floor, stylish men and women who were known to be activists or sympathizers or backers of liberal causes, among which R. D. Laing might be reckoned to belong.

Laing demonstrated a yoga eye exercise which everyone tried. Then the circle quieted down. No one spoke, waiting . . . Laing sat, adjusting the muscles of his back.

"Have you ever read Doris Lessing's *A Four-Gated City?*," asked one woman, finally. Laing said he had not. "Well, she says . . ."

"Look, why don't we talk about ourselves?," he said.

Professor Etzioni, the only person not sitting on the floor, folded his arms tightly across his chest and glared. "Why don't you?," he said.

"All right," Laing agreed, hesitating only long enough to check the source and then launching into one of his favorite stories, the one about his history of respiratory troubles in relation to his birth and childhood, ". . . sinusitis and rhinitis and tonsilitis and laryngitis and bronchitis, culminating in asthma," which he climaxed with a demonstration of truly magnificent wheezing.

"We owe it to ourselves to learn to breathe," he summed up.

Professor Etzioni was fuming. "Who cares! What makes you think anybody here is even slightly interested in your medical history? Why can't you talk about *ideas* like any civilized man? You're alleged to have a few. Perhaps you don't think they can stand by themselves . . ."

Laing didn't reply, and the rest of the party erupted into bitter quarreling.

"My God!," Laing exclaimed outside, hovering between offense and delectation over the incident, "I haven't gotten into that sort of thing for ten years, and I have *no* patience with it now. Years ago, I'd have had to go to an affair like that with an inhaler in case I got asthma. These are people who *adulate* me from a distance, but when they meet me, they can't *stand* me. I was *teaching* them about what they can do, with their eyes, their backs, their breathing. If you can produce an asthma attack at will, then that's an end of asthma. People don't realize how *important* that is. It means you've disassembled the machinery of asthma." He walked on a few steps. "Dr. Charisma! If he'd asked me what charisma was I could have told him. Max Weber said it years ago. It grows out of a group process just like that one," shaking his finger back toward the house, "where one member of the group is endowed by the others with this power or aura. I mean, of all the people there, *he* was the one who was most impressed with my charisma. He was *creating* it!"

"Have you been misunderstood?"

. Back in Suite 608 a reporter, open notebook in hand, was attempting to put his questions, trying vainly to ignore the maneuverings of the cameraman and sound man.

"I've been very much misunderstood," Laing sighed. "I spend a lot of my time trying to undo misunderstandings that are going on." He smiled noticing the young man's bemusement. "This is the first time in my life I've been given this sort of treatment."

The reporter looked skeptical. "Why, after so many years of being shy of this kind of exposure, are you laying yourself so open to it now?"

"Curiosity. And money. I'd like to get enough together to get on with it, without having to think about money. And also, having largely confined my mass-media communications to the written word, I began to get feedback about what people think I'm doing, or who they think I am, that seemed pretty far from the truth. Before, I didn't think I had the social competence to be meeting strangers and moving from one television studio to another and having cameras and tape recorders going from morning to night. I didn't think I had the balance to do it without either getting attached to it or detached from it. Now I feel I can take it or leave it. A number of years ago, I still had a bit of that insufferable intellectual superiority. I don't know whether I'd have appreciated someone like Dick Cavett, for instance . . ."

"Thank you, thank you," said Dick Cavett, holding up both hands to quell the deafening studio applause. "Let me introduce my three guests tonight, Dr. Rollo May, Dr. Nathan Kline, Director of Research at Rockland State Hospital, where he's pioneered in the use of computers and drugs in the treatment of mental illness, and Dr. R. D. Laing, who works in England and is the author of many widely acclaimed books, and who, like most people in the field, has been accused of being odd himself. Let's start here: Freud died in 1939. I assume you gentlemen will all agree about that much?"

Laing kept his eye on Kline, an impressively composed and well-informed man who could be counted on ably to defend the Goliath of institutional psychiatry against even so intrepid a David.

"How many people in America today need help?" Cavett put to them.

Kline went for it like a pro.

"That's one of my favorite questions. There was a study done in New York, where they went on a house-to-house survey, rather than waiting for people to come in. The estimate was that about twenty-three percent of the inhabitants of Manhattan were seriously enough ill to need treatment. There are about 4.2 million people in treatment at the present time in the United States. But according to these figures, there are 50 million who need it. So, in fact, we're grossly undertreated."

"Well," said Laing, "the figure in the United Kingdom is that just under fifty percent of the total hospital population of the country is made up of people in mental hospitals. So there are certainly a lot of people being treated already. And one problem I have that I don't know how Dr. Kline resolves is who, and in what state of mind, are the people who are doing the surveys, and determining who needs treatment. Because, after a while, if fifty percent of the people were to decide that the other fifty percent needed treatment, well . . ."

Kline's line was that, given the magnitude of the need, institutional psychiatry in general, and drug therapy in particular, were quicker, cheaper, and more painless, and could deal with far greater numbers than any alternative Laing could name.

Laing argued that such an approach became meaningless when you considered that the standard psychiatric criteria for diagnosing schizophrenia—a split between thinking, feeling, and behavior—applied to most people he'd ever met, including most psychiatrists.

"Even more so. Their feelings and thoughts are complete strangers to each other. And in this state of mind, they're supposed to have the competence to judge it in others, when they can't see or mend it in themselves."

Cavett smiled at Laing angelically. "Are you hurt

when you're attacked in the press for being fashion-
able and fraudulent?"

"No, but I think it's amazing the things people have
felt called upon to say about me, including that I'm a
dangerous lunatic paranoid schizophrenic, encouraging other people to get off on the same thing . . ."

"Aw, you're just imagining it," Cavett grinned. "Say,
have you ever thought you'd be better off dead?"

Laing liked that.

"How do you think you did?," I asked him.

"A draw. I effectively told several million people
that ninety-five percent of the psychiatrists in America are full of shit. That's not too bad."

It was also, apparently, what millions of people most
wanted to hear about from R. D. Laing. He was surprised. To him it was old ground, these questions of
madness and sanity. Yet madness was still the com-
manding metaphor of the times and, from the way
they talked, the reality of a great many people's lives.
They wanted a prescription, or they wanted out, or
they wanted beliefs that would stand up, or they
wanted just a little certainty—none of which Laing
could provide.

"I've always felt that my own position was actually
one of extreme skepticism, in the sense of drawing a
pretty mean limit to what it's possible to know in any
respect, and certainly to what it's possible to be certain
about."

It was the source of many of the misconceptions
about Laing's work that people failed to realize this.
They seemed to think that he was angry—he suspected
it was something in the tone of his books, although he
himself didn't read them, and hadn't written them that
way—a hectoring Jeremiah inveighing against society

and its agents (parents, psychiatrists, capitalists, Them) in their unrelenting persecution of its hapless victims (children, mental patients, workers, Us). There was something in that, he said, but it needed to be universalized. One had to see the dialectic and reciprocity in things. He'd never said that "parents are the baddies, and children are the goodies," or that the mad were sane and the sane mad, or that the family was inherently senescent or undesirable, or that the brutishness of most lives was peculiar to the capitalistic system. He knew of no general solutions, he kept repeating, or even consolations.

Yet his supporters and detractors alike, each conservative of their own received ideas, persisted in adoring or accusing him for much the same reason—namely, for holding beliefs that they either shared and approved of or that they didn't. And this is about a man to whom all received ideas are basically superstitious, who has fewer obvious beliefs than anyone I've ever met, and who claims to know virtually nothing for certain. Indeed, Laing's position, like that of any true skeptic, is, if anything, profoundly conservative. He thinks our capacities to tolerate each other's differences in behavior and states of mind are lamentably small. He thinks we interfere with each other too much. In fact, he is astonished at how flagrantly and thoughtlessly we violate each other's peace and freedom, as though we are certain about things we cannot possibly be certain about.

His argument with psychiatry is simply that the received ideas underlying it seem to him, judged either by reason or by experience, to be utterly fictitious. In theory and in practice, he finds it socially naïve, grossly unscientific to the point of superstition, and frankly indecent. This is not a new or terribly radical argument. Psychoanalysts—practitioners of the purely verbal method of treatment invented by Freud who may also, like Laing, be psychiatrists—have long objected to psychiatry on much the same grounds: that it denies the inner world, takes no account of experience except as symptomatic, and reduces people to objects.

By the medical model of mental illness, schizophrenia would appear to be some mysterious visitation that people "have" or "get," like measles or the plague. Yet unlike measles or plague, nobody has found a schizophrenia virus or bacillus to pin it on. In fact, nobody can figure out why one person "gets" it and another does not, or find any organic changes in the people who do, or detect any clear genetic pattern to its incidence in families, or even agree about when or how to diagnose it. Indeed, nobody really has the slightest idea what schizophrenia *is,* if it's anything at all. The only thing that is known for sure is that some people—millions of them—appear from the rather queer viewpoint of normality to have queer experiences and to behave in queer ways: that is, they say, see, hear, feel, or do things that most other people don't.

Nevertheless, largely on the basis of the discomfort these other people feel about anything queer, a psychiatrist can invoke the magical notion of schizophrenia, confine someone to a hospital, and subject him to various persuasions, subtle and not so subtle, such as (mainly) drugging him into tranquillity or (more rarely these days) shocking him into forgetfulness, or even removing odd bits of his brain, until he stops saying, seeing, hearing, feeling, or doing whatever it is that's so queer. And all this is done with the best of intentions for the patient's own good.

This is not to say that the mad are actually sane, or in some higher state, or best left to their schizophrenia.

Schizophrenia literally means *broken-hearted*. But the heartbreak, the feelings of terror and despair are not "caught," they are the result of terrifying experiences and desperate circumstances—often family situations, rather common ones, of a type that Laing calls "double-binds," in which, without conscious malice, one person is repeatedly subjected to simultaneous, absolutely contradictory injunctions and attributions about who he is, or how he feels or what he thinks, until he can no longer tell who he is, or what he feels or thinks. This is a perfectly real persecution unto psychological death. Yet if a woman complains to a psychiatrist that her husband is trying to kill her, or if she acts as though she had already been murdered, the psychiatrist, who does not see her husband following her around with a mean look and deadly weapon (in fact, her husband is probably the "nice guy" who brought her in), will conclude that she is suffering from a paranoid delusion. Laing maintains that to judge such a person's behavior as deluded or inappropriate or insane, when in terms of her own experience it may be perfectly intelligible, is a barbarous nonsense. Furthermore, it's hard to imagine any more effective ways of confirming paranoia than by trying to put a stop to it by the usual psychiatric methods which are so exactly counterproductive that she might be better left alone to get on with "going mad."

He does not say this lightly. He suggests that if we are unaware of how mad we are, we are even less aware of how mad we *need* to be; that madness may be a natural healing process of the mind in which the unbearable contradictions of experience begin to break down. Instead of being interrupted under conditions of near-penal confinement by psychiatrists who see it as queer and scary, this process ought to be guided and sanctioned, given genuine refuge and asylum among sympathetic people with experience of such frightening inner journeys. Or, at least, there should be the choice. To embark on such a journey—to go mad, in Laing's sense—is to give up all certainty, to lose all distinctions one has ever made between real and not real, good and bad, here and there, now and then, you and not-you. Some people might understandably prefer forgetfulness. Yet clinging to these profoundly "uncertain" certainties may be at the root of all our madness, schizophrenics and normals alike. And he intimates that for those who are willing, or whom terror and despair compel, there is the possibility for rebirth at the end of such a journey into an existence far more sane than the one understood by normality. Just how to go about it, or be guided to go about it, is a subject on which Laing has so far been mostly silent, for to define true sanity would necessitate speaking of matters for which the only developed language currently available is religious or poetic.

The subject came up one evening at a dinner party given by Laing's New York publisher. Conversation turned to his hopes of establishing a global string of asylum communities where people who needed to could go thoroughly mad, and a training center for therapists where he would make himself available. A young analyst asked just what sort of therapy Laing proposed and whether he had abandoned orthodox psychoanalysis altogether. Laing replied that a *therapist*, in the original sense of the word derived from the Greek, was an attendant, and as such should be a specialist in attentiveness and awareness. That was also the object of certain Buddhist meditative traditions: to cultivate equal awareness of mental, emotional, social, and physical experience, the Four Foundations of Mindfulness.

"I've been studying that for fifteen years and I've long wished to see it developed as a basis for psychotherapy. The trouble is that it's very hard to find people with a flair for this sort of thing. It takes years. Yet it seems to me that it's a prerequisite of being a therapist to be equally attentive to all four parts of the puzzle. You can't just take one and blow it up as though it were the whole thing. You ought to be flexible enough with someone, for instance, to decide to deal with some things as a social phenomenon, with others as physical, recommending this or that exercise —a three-day fast, for example—or be strictly analytical and so on. For lack of a better term, you could call that psychoanalysis."

"Do you still use the couch?"

"No. I see a few people individually once or twice a week in my home. They sit wherever they feel comfortable, on a mattress or on the floor or in a chair, and I generally mirror them."

"For fifty minutes?"

"I've abandoned that. My own analyst often used to cut me off in mid-sentence if the hour was up, and he didn't like it if I looked at my watch. He said I was trying to control the session. I didn't complain. If those were the rules of his game, I could play. But I really think most of the rules of analysis are more for the analyst's benefit than the patient's, for without those controls, he might freak out, not know who or where he was. But that's the risk if he wants to do psychoanalysis."

"That puts a tremendous burden on the analyst," I commented. "He has to be in a very special state of mind."

"That's how any analyst ought to be! That's what being an analyst is all about! And it shouldn't be a burden to him either. He should be doing that any time, effortlessly and completely willingly."

Any time? You mean, not just in the office cemented behind the couch, but in real life, too? Maybe, I thought, we're getting to it, the thing about this man that people find so out of the ordinary. For the state of mind he is so casually recommending is no everyday occurrence, no ordinary state of attentiveness picked up at your local psychoanalytic institute. People who are habitually in it have usually been called saints or buddhas, rarely psychoanalysts. The Buddhists call this state of mind "perfect mindfulness." W. R. Bion (1970), an analyst Laing greatly admires, calls it "o" —absolute zero. Bion says that for psychoanalysis to approach to the condition of true science, the analyst must divest himself of attachment to all memory, all desire, and all attempts at ordinary understanding. This is not the same as forgetting or denying reality, for the reality sought in analysis—psychic or mental reality—is quite different from the external sensory reality of which all memories and desires are constituted and which is properly the object of other sciences. It involves relaxing one's hold, one's identification with all such particulars until one is as nearly as possible universal, infinite, without a self. According to Bion, that the patient even recognizes his analyst from one day to the next as a particular person is an impediment to analysis. Only at absolute zero can the analyst be at one with the reality of his patient; it is a sort of negative capability, by which the analyst gets to know his patient by *becoming* him.

"And the analyst isn't *having* that experience," Laing continued, "he *is* it, completely identified with it, without the superimposition upon it of past constructions or projections into the future or mental fabrications of any kind. No recall and no forgetting. He is simply absorbed in the present of that particular relationship. That seems to me to be as much the object of mysticism or the practice of spiritual disciplines as of psychoanalysis; the revealing of the phenomena that one has before one, like the situation in this room right now, through sight, sound, taste, touch, smell, and body sensibility, unobscured by any superimposed constructions. And that goes for any situation."

Laing scanned his audience briefly for signs of understanding—these were not easy matters—and in the silence that followed, decided to backtrack to the more familiar approach.

"See, I'm against rigor that comes from mechanism, like clock time. I'm sure, internally, we have a very fine sense of time. At some level we must be aware of each passing moment, and counting them. Rigor ought to be real, not mechanical. I tell people to turn up early morning or midday or midafternoon, just referring to the times of day. In practice they get to know that I'll see them for about an hour and a half. And I don't stand for any nonsense. I push them as far and as hard as they can stand, or are willing and able in the time, and I'll interrupt if it goes on too long."

He hesitated.

"I couldn't have done all this a few years ago. I couldn't have handled it. I'm also much more didactic than I ever was before—I'll tell someone it'd be good if they tried not eating, for instance. But what difference does it make whether I see people in my bathrobe or even if one of my children walks in? Since it's in my home anyway, people are bound to pick up a certain amount of family noise."

The young analyst hemmed—psychoanalysts were

supposed to be anonymous and nondirective. That was the theory.

"Can you still get the transference neurosis?"

"Of course you do! That's the main thing!"

Transference, the very basis of psychoanalysis, refers to the process by which the analyst, by his detachment and anonymity—his refusal to play along with his patient's preconceptions or expectations—creates the novel situation in which, appearing to have no self, he is given one by his disconcerted patient who concocts it out of his own feelings and fantasies and early memories. Laing appeared to be neither anonymous nor nondirective with his patients, and yet he claimed to get transference. It was tempting to suppose the very same process might be behind the extravaganza of his fame, not with a few patients in the privacy of his living room, but any time, all the time, out there in the world, at a distance, among thousands.

I decided to prod him a little. "Don't you really think it's going to make a difference? The more your patients know about you personally, the less they can use you as a reasonably reliable reflection of their own states of mind. Freud said . . ."

"They still don't *know* me! They may think they know something, but they still don't know whether I'm a good person, whether I'm trustworthy, whether I'm poisonous. What do they know?"

The young analyst, still persevering, asked about regression—how in situations of great stress people revert to earlier and more primitive states of mind. Controlled regression with maximal verbalization is the classical model of psychoanalysis. Laing's idea that psychotics may be best served by being helped to go thoroughly mad is a more radical version of the same therapeutic principle.

"What about the Ten-Day Voyage in *The Politics of*

Experience?" (Laing, 1967), asked the analyst, referring to the famous account of the healing psychotic
episode of Jesse Watkins. "Did you propose that as
a model?"

"Certainly not as a model of the natural time such
things take, or as a scenario for people to follow. In
fact, I've known of only two or three such experiences
that people have actually had through to completion.
Otherwise, I've seen it in bits and pieces, here and
there. But I guess I do have a model in mind. I'm just
positive there is a process involved in regression that
has never been adequately investigated or described.
In fact, my next book will be about that, a sort of perceptual calculus whose first principle might be 'Let
there be a distinction.' Then it's a matter of describing
how, going both ways, we either accumulate distinctions into a composable picture of the world, or work
back, by reversion, to the zero point. You see, I think
regression, as a mechanism of psychosis, may well be
that process of shedding distinctions. And it can happen either explosively, in which case it leads to chaos
and confusion, or systematically, in which case it can
be a very good thing. But there are so many ways
people can get lost. Controlled regression, even in
analysis, is not always so easy. People can explode.
I've often had the experience of watching someone
go crazy right before my eyes, very quickly. Suddenly
there is an explosion of anger and spite and envy
directed against the operations of one's own mind,
sending fragments into the farthest reaches of mental
space. Sometimes I've felt they were long overdue
for it. I couldn't imagine how they'd held out for as
long as they had."

Later that week a group of injured-looking souls—
outpatients or former inmates of mental hospitals and

their friends to whom any such talk of madness was far from academic—huddled silently together in a classroom at the State University of New York at Stonybrook, waiting for the room to clear out. A crowd of students jostled each other, curious to see Laing, and a few brave ones asked questions. He answered quietly, warmly, addressing himself directly to each petitioner and frequently answering to what he sensed they meant but had not asked. At last only the group of pale ones remained. They had news for him. At the nearby state hospital experiments were being done with wrist sensors and electrodes implanted into the brains of chronic patients, as a means of monitoring them at long distance and immobilizing them at the flip of a switch should the sensors register signs of excitement that a central computer read as portending dangerous behavior. What could he tell them? Laing shook his head sadly.

"Take care of each other."

Two more sectors of Laing's fame remained to be explored, two major parties of constituents I had yet to watch him meet, the mystics and the revolutionaries, who on the whole do not see eye to eye. The mystics materialized one afternoon in the person of Oscar Ichazo, spiritual master of the Arica Institute, named after the town in Chile where he'd been found by a group of Americans who had persuaded him to come and impart his teachings—a synopticon of assorted disciplines based largely on the teachings of Gurdjieff—to the spiritually needy and ready citizens of New York.

"New York City contains more people prepared for reality than the world has previously seen in one culture," Oscar was quoted as saying in a full-page ad in *The New York Times*.

Composed and meticulously expressionless as a cat, Oscar removed his shoes and settled into one corner of the sofa, while Laing lay loosely crouched in the other, scowling amiably. They spoke ramblingly of mantras and yogas and techniques of meditation, of phenomenology and skepticism and the ancient Greeks, of drugs and reincarnation, of the sixteen lives of Karmapa and the present one of Chögyam Trungpa, a Tibetan *tulku* of their acquaintance.

"Anyway, we are living in a very impressive time," affirmed Oscar, rolling to a point his account of "The Work" as he referred to Arica. Now three hundred strong in New York and San Francisco, the whole school —after two years of intensive work on their minds and bodies that often went on for ten to sixteen hours a day—was about to set out laying what was called the "Open Path" on an unsuspecting (or suspecting) nation. Oscar's face broke into a visionary smile.

"More than impressive, really. An unbelievable time! Things are going to happen now, very soon. And I guess this is the story of the entire planet. It is a matter of season, really. We are changing season, and in a very spectacular way. It is spring! You know, spring comes, and nobody knows where it was before."

Oscar had gone, and Laing lay on the sofa, his eyes shut.

"So is spring upon us, do you think?," I asked.

"I really don't know about these things any better than anyone else, whether it's all fantasy or not. One has the impression that sort of thing is spreading. There are a few people everywhere who are prepared to put people through these numbers, a complete system of practices. But I certainly couldn't say to anyone that if you come to me, in two years time you'll have moved your body and mind to a completely different place that you can't even imagine—a complete mutation physically, mentally, spiritually—and that for the first time in your life you will *know*. On the other hand, for anyone who actually goes through something like that, month after month of doing nothing but mental and physical exercises, well, it's bound to do something. It would put anyone's mind in rather a different place, certainly not the same as people who hadn't."

"But will it save the planet?," I asked. "You realize that's Oscar's goal?"

"It's a tremendously powerful thing, a group like that. He's setting up a string of self-multiplying bodies of which each person is a cell. And they can all share and distribute among them the energy going through the whole system. They're all chanting and dancing and praying together. Any work they do is entirely incidental. It's their whole lives. Well, it's a different way of spending your life than having a glass of brandy and a cigar after a heavy meal and watching television. I suppose some people need to have some sort of ideology or mythology to justify doing that sort of thing, but what it actually means is that they manage to get together and sing and dance, which is marvelous. There have been enormous movements like that in the past. In the thirties there was Yogananda's Self-Realization movement, and the Gurdjieff movement with Ouspensky and Bennet, and Subud, and Scientology, and the Theosophists. And look at that book by Norman Cohn (1970), *The Pursuit of the Millennium*. The world's coming to an end, salvation, realization, redemption by one's own efforts up to a point, by the grace of God finally, but you've got to show an earnest of your desire. Or the early Christians —the descent of the dove, the speaking in tongues, the ESP, the telepathy, the wonders and miracles. And all this is taken to be miraculous only by the ignorant.

It's just natural law that is beyond our comprehension." Laing turned toward me and frowned. "What about you? Do you believe in these things, or disbelieve, or know, or don't know, or know you don't know, or . . ."

"I don't know. I do my best. I go through one posture and then another . . ."

"As far as I'm concerned, they're all postures—belief, nonbelief, certainty, all of them. It's all the mind's throwing up one structure after another. I can't see any purpose in it. It's just what the mind seems to do. I still try to describe these operations, but I don't give them very much value. They're shadows. In a way, I've moved from the most serious position in regard to these things to the most frivolous, regarding them more for their aesthetic value than for their truth. And even that's misleading." He was silent for some minutes. Then, suddenly: "But I have, through meditation, had the experience of real stillness. It was very refreshing."

Refreshing? What about bliss, divinity, ecstasy, the absolute, getting out of here? Refreshment you can get from Ballantine. But bliss? That's what people wanted to know from R. D. Laing. Half America would give anything for it, and the other half simply hadn't heard about it yet. I mean, he'd been there, Ceylon, India. . . . .

"We're all curious about your stay in Ceylon and India last year."

We were in the director's office of the William Alanson White Institute of Psychiatry, New York's transactional school of psychoanalysis. Laing had just been greeted by the five senior analysts, heartily and a little nervously, as though he might have been the reincarnation of the institute's founding genius, Harry

Stack Sullivan. During his previous visit in 1967 he
had talked about how distortions in perception and
experience are generated and perpetuated in all of us,
mad and sane alike, and about the intelligibility of
madness and the intolerant irrationality of its treatment, suggesting that schizophrenia, on the evidence,
might be no more than a punitive name that some
people give other people whose behavior or viewpoints
disturb them. No one had been able to regard the
schizophrenic process in quite the same way since,
they all said. Laing listened carefully, wondering what
was on their minds now. It was the same thing, apparently, that was on all their patients' minds as well,
namely bliss, and whether what Laing said—or what
people guessed he said—was really true, that if you
really, seriously, went completely crazy . . .

"We're all curious . . ."

There was a long silence during which Laing
combed his fingers through his hair, pursed his lips,
sighed, scowled, his eyes darting to and fro while his
face made one apparition after another. It was a long,
wayward story. As a boy of fourteen or fifteen he'd
had a religious experience of conversion, a compelling
sense that he'd been saved by the grace of God. But
that sense eventually gave way to another, scientific
and atheistic, that the religious position was a projection of the mind, one of its archaic deposits. And that
position led to yet another, agnostic and convulsed
with interminable questions. What is the truth, or is
there a truth? Is there any certainty? Or if there are
no absolutes, are there at least beliefs that are relatively more true than others, and if not, is one then
prepared to abdicate the light of reason and dissolve
into a complete relativism in which anything goes? Or
is the mind, as Ludwig Wittgenstein suggested, be-

mused by language, entrapped like a fly in a bottle, vainly struggling to map the whole cosmos through a haze of words? And what is to be done, or is anything to be done? Is the idea that something can be done a part of the sickness of the mind? He went on calmly, smiling, scarcely pausing for punctuation.

"So my mind kept veering round, entertaining positions that in some way it couldn't see were in some sort of error. I was in the position of a psychotic who recognized that he was perhaps psychotic or deluded, but couldn't specify what the delusion was, and no one else could tell him. Then one reads the books, goes window-shopping—the Hindu traditions, the southern Buddhists, the Mahayana, the Tibetans, Chan, Zen, the Sufis—and one finds them all saying, in effect, that in whatever society or time or place one is born into, in this era of the world's history, which they call the 'age of darkness,' one's mind, in its ordinary state, is obscured in some way. One can't see things as they really are. You can't tell what's the matter with your mind, they say, but you can take it from us that its in a very disastrously confused state indeed. Whatever you take to be real is, in fact, not real, and you can't appeal to statistics, because 99.99 percent of people are in the same state. Well, however implausible that strikes you, it has a very disturbing effect on your system. As the Sufis describe it, your eyes become sunken, you lose weight, you can't sleep, you can't think of anything else, you lose interest in sex, you become disgusted with all sensations, you don't want to see or hear anything, and everything becomes a burden and a complication that is more than you can cope with. All your mind wants is to be free of its own operations. They call this the dust on the mirror. The idea, then, is to wipe the dust off, to get clear mirror wisdom. This can only arise when there's a total suspension of all input, and the mind is concentrated on one object—one point—until all else falls away. It's like an abscess that must take its course until it bursts. Quite a lot of people go psychotic in the process. Or they give up and become cranks. Anyway, I thought my mind could do with a rest. It's tired. I've been at it for quite a number of years, right from the Greek irregular verbs at school, through university, and into psychiatry, through psychoanalysis, reading a lot and writing, and listening to people for ten hours a day, starting one marriage and having children and breaking up and starting another marriage and having more children. Well, I looked at all this, and I wasn't at the end of my tether exactly, but I thought it was definitely time to change the scene, take a rest, look at another culture, and so . . ."

He went to Ceylon and studied Satipatthana meditation, the Four Foundations of Mindfulness, which seemed the most congenial of the traditional practices he'd come across. There was nothing especially mystical about it, it required no particular beliefs, was without ritual, was consistent with his notion of what psychoanalysis was really about, and it did, in fact, calm his mind considerably, at least for a time.

And then, in India, he fell in with a fifty-one-year-old swami, an M.D. from New Delhi who spoke fluent English, French, and Hindi and who, at twenty-nine, when he felt that his mind "was going ahead of itself" as he put it, had abandoned city life and his medical practice and for seven and a half years wandered naked in jungle and mountain retreats, never seeing the face of another human being. These days he lived on a mountain under an overhanging rock, an hour's walk from the nearest village, attired in a loincloth and the traditional ocher-colored robe of an Indian who has renounced the world. Laing visited him there for a month.

"His company had an extraordinary effect of putting my mind at rest. You see, how I construe this business of a mystical quest is that there's a schema of being contained within the world. The world is experienced as a container in which one is. Ontogenetically, the deepest resonance of that would be the intrauterine state, which one has both a longing and a nostalgia to get back to and an idealization of. And along with this sense of being contained goes a feeling that one has in some way to get out of it—not to get out of one's society or relationships, but to get out of one's habits of thought, one's use of words, one's habitual postures and movements. So one might use yoga exercises or Sufi dancing to try to get out of the body, or meditative exercises to get out of one's habitual state of mind, or . . . anything to get out of it. All of which reinforces the central metaphor, that one is to be reborn. One feels enclosed and entrapped, and all one's efforts to get out, every additional thought about it, only seem to make it worse, seem to be digging one's grave. As the Greeks put it, one's body is both the womb and the grave of the soul. And so long as we identify with it, we're stuck.

"For instance, one instruction I was given by the monks in Ceylon was to think of myself as a puppet, to think of every movement, all in painfully slow motion, before making it. Now that induces a state of mind that we would regard as an extreme schizoid state, cultivating disaffiliation, disidentification, with the body. . . . Well, it was very interesting to do that, but I'd never go around recommending it. I'm sure it would drive some people completely crazy. But what seemed to be involved was an attempt to shell oneself

out of the body, like a pea out of a pod, so one's no
longer identified with any form or shape, any bit of it,
or the whole of it, or none of it. Doing that, one sometimes experiences major shifts of mind, like avalanches.
In the course of a few hours one traverses positions like
absolute subjectivist idealism, where one can literally
see that the world is nothing but a flower in the sky,
a mirage in the desert; and then that would pass, and
the scene would change into everything being exactly
as it is, and the former position would now appear to
be nonsense, and so on. Finally, the way I construed
the etiology of mystical experience is that it seems to
be a mapping onto mental constructions of a very
complex regressive and progressive womb fantasy.
You seem to have a sort of birth experience, on a
mental level. First it seems pretty hopeless and de-
spairing—there's no future, no movement, you're not
getting anywhere. And then you start to get somewhere, but you don't know where, don't know whether
it's forward or backward. And, finally, a light begins
to dawn at the end of the tunnel, the abscess or bubble
bursts, and you're out of it. Except as soon as you're
out of it, you're back in it—you're in the world again,
and once more the mountains are mountains, the sky
is a sky, and a river is a river, and you wonder, *What
has that *all* been about?"*

Whatever it might be about, it seemed pretty clear
to Steve Roday, a Movement journalist I'd met at the
Mailer show and who turned up one afternoon in Suite
608, shaking with that inexplicable fear, that it was no
good for the revolution that R. D. Laing had gone
mystical. Still, you couldn't be sure about him, there
were so many conflicting stories, maybe it wasn't so, or
if it was, maybe . . .

Figuring that to be crazy and a revolutionary was bound to be a good line to the great man's sympathies, Roday tried it:

"Yeah, I've had my freak-outs, but when you do freak out, you really see an awful lot that you don't see otherwise—you know, power things, people controlling people . . ."

It was a mistake. Whether on account of the immediate prospect of having to disabuse the Movement, in the person of Roday, of some of its fonder expectations concerning "revolutionary hero" R. D. Laing, or some more mysterious psychoalchemy altogether, at the sight of Roday sweating and fairly quaking with nerves, Laing appeared ineffably to have mutated. His voice went up, he craned forward instead of slouching, his eyes flashed, and, compared to the meandering and the unassuming diffidence of previous days, he was brisk, snappy, argumentative.

"That's a generalization which you have to balance with the other one—that sometimes you see a lot less. I've never thought that the generality of people who are freaked out are in some higher state of illumination than the average, ordinary person. I guess I tend to get impatient with people who freak out over that —they see how people are devouring and mangling and controlling each other, and they think they're into the complete opposite. Actually, I'd very much like to meet some of these powerful characters who appear to be in control. I only make personal judgments about people I've met personally. I might make a political judgment, or a judgment on the scale of good and evil. . . ."

"You're not foreclosing on political judgments?"

"How could I? There used to be an old liberal dictum that what is politically right cannot be morally wrong. Well, I don't believe that. A political judgment is concerned only with power—how to acquire it, how to maintain it, and how to enhance it once one's got it. The right political judgment is the judgment that enhances your power and diminishes the next person's. In that sense, whether a war is justifiable or not depends purely on the political parameters—your power and their power—to be resorted to only if you think you can win . . . Looking at it that way, I don't know what one would say about Vietnam."

"You don't know?"

"No. But there's another sort of judgment, about good and evil. At one extreme there's a question whether *all* politics isn't evil and immoral. Or whether there's such a thing as a necessary evil. Or—"

"You know, to the people who are going to read this, this conversation with R. D. Laing is going to sound like the Pentagon Papers."

"Then you're not listening. You've granted every point I've made, right?"

"Yeah, I wouldn't fight 'em."

"So?"

"So I'm trying to lead you out of it, basically. I feel in a vacuum. I can't even get you to respond to the war as weird and bad and—"

"Yes, yes, yes, of course I agree it's weird. It's weird, and it's terrifying."

"Listen, the question is, how are we going to deal with power?"

"Well, how? How are you going about it?"

"By working from inside existing institutions and building counterinstitutions, by propagandizing the idea that politics isn't mystical, that technology isn't mystifying. . . . I mean, we're breaking our goddamn teeth, we're looking for advice, we're changing every day so we can cope, we're trying not to freak out . . ."

"So you're keeping yourselves in good order."

"No, not in good order, man. You can't stay in good order in a struggle like this. *We* don't know how to do it. What ideas do *you* have? A lot of the people who read your books are interested in political struggle, right? Well, what do you have to say to them?"

Laing grew quiet and solemn. "I don't see any way whereby one can take power without overpowering the people who have it with more power. So by the same token that one judges their power to be evil, ours would be a greater evil. And I don't think it's a matter of opinion. I think it's a mathematical certainty: All power corrupts, and absolute power currupts absolutely. One would necessarily become more corrupt than they, because I just don't see how it could possibly be peaceful. Are you prepared to arm yourself, or to support an armed struggle—a full-scale civil war in America?" He looked at Roday. "You think I'm just splitting hairs."

"Or just opting out of judgments that may involve action."

Laing gave a huge sigh. "Look, let's take the magnification of my image in America. Two years ago, before I went to India, I was told by a professor at the University of Florida that ninety-five percent of the professors of psychiatry in America regarded me as schizophrenic. Now these are the people charged with the system of mind control in this country. Even if they themselves don't know it, structurally and functionally they are the agents of a very intricate set of controls. Their job, effectively, is to allow only those states of mind to manifest themselves that aren't a danger to national security, in the largest sense. And the system extends right into the marrow of our bones, to our endocrine functions, our posture, our schemata of perception, the rhythm of our lives, our use of language. It even presides over our births, how we're born. Now the only way many people know to get their minds out of state control is to freak out, to go out of control. But there are other ways, like the ones I've practiced, which don't involve freaking out. I know that's not the image most people have of me, left or right. But they've got to *meet* me to disabuse themselves. It's possible I could teach them a lesson: to meet someone whose mind is out of control but who can speak in a perfectly plain, urbane manner, who, in other words, is in a position to examine the system of controls without freaking out at the sight of it. This is my contribution to the revolution: to learn how to dismantle that bit of state control from within, because you're not going to dismantle it from without. It means you've got to get *to* the minds of the people in control to see if they can be changed. Of course, a lot of psychiatrists think an idea like that is itself evidence of schizophrenia. That's what they *call* schizophrenia. But the people in power aren't getting away with it either. They're in the power of the power that they wield more than most people. In that sense the black in Harlem is still a bit more out of control than the successful businessman's son at West Point."

Laing looked questioningly at Roday, who shook his head with evident approval.

"Now although I'm not primarily talking to the converted on this tour, the fact is some of the converted have also got fairly confused. A lot of what they take to be revolutionary concepts manifest the characteristics of the very control system they're fighting. And they may have to give some things up. I'm not telling them how to pursue the particular struggle they're in, they can best gauge that themselves. But, for instance, there are very few people around who've made it in terms of even so basic a thing as their bodies. If one's decided to start, the first thing to start with is oneself— one's own mind, own body, own room, own family, own friends. And that's *not* a subjectivist, schizoid, withdrawn, antirevolutionary cop-out." Roday looked worried again. Laing said, "Can you justify any act of repression?"

"Yeah, if the results are for the good."

"Oh, *God!*," Laing wailed. "It's like saying that to produce an exquisitely beautiful form of movement, as the Chinese did, you'd cripple the feet of your children. I find it difficult to suppose that anyone could be an effective revolutionary without having mastered the contributions of Marx, Freud, and Darwin. But Marx was an enormously alienated man. One of his children died of pneumonia and starvation because he wouldn't deign to spend a few hours a week writing articles. One's got to take that into consideration before one considers him an example to emulate. Having seen that, I'd expect any present-day revolutionary not to fuck up his own family in the course of pursuing his revolutionary interests. And I wouldn't trust entirely the large-scale vision of a man who had such an area of blindness. Any Marxism I subscribed to would have to include among its essential, primary aims the setting of one's own family aright, and not doing one at the expense of the other. Again and again I see the lives and the families of so-called revolutionaries are as screwed up as any you can imagine. If they're going to be serious, they're going to have to stop that.

"And they're not going to stop it without first being able to *see* it. And they're not *seeing* it. The visibility of social events is *nil!* All these views and abstractions that empower one's conduct must be derived ultimately from the raw sense-data we receive, so we're going to have to improve our sense-data apparatus—how we see, hear, stand, sit, sleep. The endocrine system, muscles, appetites, fantasies, memories, these all have to be disencumbered. People think that's a form of self-indulgence, of bourgeois idealism, of wasting time away from the struggle. But that's a misconception about what the revolution is. It's not going to stop one doing anything one's doing. It'll only enable one to *see* what one's doing. What's the point of gaining all the temporal power in the world if one loses one's own mind in the process?"

The New York leg of the tour was almost over, and I would soon be leaving. It was after two o'clock one morning, and Laing was sitting on the floor in Suite 608 in a terry-cloth bathrobe. It seemed to me just the time for philosophy.

"So, what do you think about fame, Ronnie?"

"Fame is 'that last infirmity of noble mind,'" he quoted from Milton's *Lycidas,* and for a few minutes he was silent. "I suppose what that means is that fame is the last thing seducing the noble mind into pursuing worldly aims rather than recognizing its true ones, which are unworldly—the last symptom of the mind's disease. I don't know what others Milton listed, but I suppose there'd be the pursuit of power, the pursuit of wealth, the pursuit of family, meaning relationships that one can both control and depend upon, and the last one to go is fame. It's got nothing in particular to do with wealth, or with power—one might be famous for being a saint. And it's got nothing to do with relationships, because one might be prepared to sacrifice all that for fame. Fame is the most subtle. In a way it's the most innocent, too, because you're not taking advantage of anyone, you're not transgressing or trespassing, you're not doing any harm. You just want other people to know you and remember you. So you make a deal with fortune: you'll be good enough or bad enough, you'll work for it . . . and I suppose fame can sometimes be thrust upon you," he added quietly.

"What's the point?," asked Danny Halperin, who lay stretched out on the sofa. "Just so people will know you?"

"Immortality. To prolong and amplify and multiply an image one can identify with is the nearest thing on this earth to the eternal. A lot of people aren't prepared to settle for being an anonymous grain of sand which happens to be part of a named stretch of seashore. The Greeks regarded fame as the most honorable of human motives. In Homer the hero will die for it, to be remembered.

"Can that be from a worldly preoccupation? When it comes to fame, it becomes spiritualized somehow. There's a spiritual narcissism—one wants to be higher up the spiritual hierarchy, a bit nearer to the center of the cosmic real estate. One wants at least to be among the cherubim or seraphim, or near the throne itself, sitting at the right hand of the Father, or the Father himself, omnipotent, omniscient, and so on. I remember Sartre used to say in the old days that man's aim, his impossible passion, was to be God. Perhaps fame is the subtlest form of that. I mean, when you consider it, apart from just standing and walking and breathing and so forth, what's the point of doing anything?"

"Maybe the danger in pursuing fame is like the danger Plato saw in art," I suggested. "It closely feigns the truth but isn't."

"It comes closest," Laing agreed. "I suppose the desire for it is just part of being human, like sin, or evil, or worldliness, as that term was once used. 'Created frail, commanded to be sound.'—that's the vision. 'There is no health; Physicians say that we, at best, enjoy but a neutrality. And can there be worse sickness, than to know that we are never well, nor can be so?' John Donne, 'An Anatomy of the World.' That's a very strong mood," Laing sighed.

"And what," I asked, "has been *your* relationship to this subtlest of human motivations?"

"Oh, I was very much motivated by the whole fame complex, especially in my teens," Laing grinned. "I never was sure what it was for, but I used to compare the lives of famous intellectuals or writers to see when they produced their first books. I noted that Havelock Ellis, for instance, decided when he was nineteen that he'd publish his first book by the time he was thirty. And I adopted that. I saw to it that I'd finished *The Divided Self* by then. There's sort of a competition, too, in terms of status and weight and who figures most in the *Dictionary of National Biography* and whether one would exchange the fame of this person for the fame of that one. There are some rather tawdry claims to fame." Laing started to laugh. "Or the question of what sort of fame you want—the fame of a successful general, or a president of the United States, or a Nobel Prize winner in geophysics on some point that will be remembered for a long, long time."

"What sort did you decide on?"

"Oh, the fame of a wise man."

"Why?"

"Well, since I wanted to be wise, and I wanted to be famous, I thought I might as well be famous for being wise . . . *and* wise to see the vanity of all that."

"And how did you go about it?"

"Oh, I consciously pursued both," Laing confessed, gasping with laughter. "And in an equally calculated manner. I was very peculiar, from very early on. I decided at the age of thirteen, for instance, that I would make a point of never forgetting anything that was painful. I haven't met anyone with a mind quite like mine. It's somewhat original.

"But I'm famous at a more popular level than what I'd been playing for. I mean, to crown my career by delivering a series of Gifford Lectures that would be a sort of classic, like a sutra or the *Four Quartets* for the last half of the twentieth century—"

"That was your goal?," Danny asked.

"That was definitely one of them," Laing said. "It's not quite what I bargained for, my fame. It's something I've had to adjust to. . . . It's even been proposed to me by the boys that this is just a dry run on the small circuit, and if I get really professional at it by the end, they figure I can come back and storm the Plaza or something. Then I'll be worth as much as Liza Minelli, and I can do a late-night cabaret . . ."

"Ah, me, witness the infirmity of a noble mind," I moaned.

Laing smiled and sighed. "I can only do what I take to be my best, or else just give it all up. I've certainly arrived at a position now where fame, as far as I can see, looking at it as hard as I can, really means nothing to me at all. It's just fantasy, sheer fantasy. What's the point of putting oneself out just for the hell of being known? I've never really seen any point in it. But then I've done quite a number of things in my life that I didn't see any point in. In fact, I've seldom seen the point in doing anything. But that's never stopped me from doing quite a lot. I suppose the next step is actu-

ally to give it up. In India I met a saint whom I asked
what he thought my next step in life should be. He
said I should either stay with him or go back and
spread the true religion. In its most ample definition I
take that to be simply telling people what one regards
as the truth, as far as one can say it. I think one of the
reasons for all the hemming and hawing in my per-
formance is that I don't really know what to talk about.
If I launched into an exposition of the First Noble
Truth of the Buddha, for instance, I don't feel I could
take any money for it. If I can make enough bread and
get sufficiently practiced, then I'll do that, if that's the
way it goes. Meanwhile, I think it's fair enough to
work my way into it, taking on humbler but no less
important assignments. The whole psychiatric bit
bothers people a great deal, although I'm a bit bored
by it myself. Really I should use that boredom to get
into it with more facility."

"Maybe fame has its uses," I said. "Do you have any
sense that you've been called?"

I was referring, as Laing recognized, to an idea of
Bion's, the analyst whose work he so much admires.

> The "exceptional individual" may be variously de-
> scribed as a genius, a messiah, a mystic, and his following
> may be large or small . . . The mystic may declare him-
> self as a revolutionary or he may claim that his function is
> to fulfill the laws, conventions, and destiny of his group.
> It would be surprising if any true mystic were not re-
> garded by the group as a mystical nihilist at some stage
> of his career and by a greater or lesser proportion of the
> group. It would be equally surprising if he were not in
> fact nihilistic to some group if for no other reason than
> that the nature of his contribution is certain to be de-
> structive of the laws, conventions, culture, and therefore
> coherence, of a group within the group, if not of the
> whole group. In this it is evident that the character of

the group cannot be excluded from the facts of the evolution of a mystic in a group.

"Yes, I've felt for some time that I'm being put in a
certain position," Laing replied, "that I'm a sort of
light heavyweight, if not quite a heavyweight, being
put up to represent something. People are saying, 'You
speak for us.' They're not especially listening to me.
They just want to hear what they take to be the decent
thing, the honest thing, the human thing, the thing
that's still going, isn't broken down, is still alive. One
way and another, they've decided to back my perform-
ance."

He waved toward a pile of books and papers on the
desk.

"Look at that. Those are all things people have sent,
information, things they've found, the best of this or
that, whether it's on Tantra or nuclear physics."

"You've got a big organization working for you," I
observed. Laing laughed. "Yeah, a big organization
. . . In a way I'm treated like a sort of queen bee.
They put the juice into me and then hope I can come
out with the right stuff."

He paused and stifled a laugh. "Only too glad to," he
smiled. "I'd be delighted to."

"You want a single spot?," asked the stage manager
of Hunter College's cavernous auditorium. "Sure, you
can have whatever you want. When you walk out here
tonight, you're an actor!"

The consensus on the Hunter talk was that it was a
bust and a rip-off. Laing had no idea when he left for
the auditorium what he was going to say, and, being
shy of large crowds and determined in any event not
to lecture, he sat, looking rather lonely and unhappy,

barefoot and cross-legged on a silken rug in the light of a single spot, and told stories, haphazardly—whatever came into his mind.

"I hope you won't be disappointed," he began. "A number of people I've met in the last week have become a little bewildered, sometimes seriously, and perplexed and confused quite quickly on meeting me. Or so it seemed. Because what they met wasn't what they expected."

He sighed a lot and hemmed and hawed and spoke of his uncertainty.

"I am a student of my own nature," he said. "I can only tell you how my own life has gone. It's been a very circuitous journey. I certainly would not propose it as a model for anyone else to follow. In a sense, I suppose it's just the story of a mid-twentieth-century intellectual. I suppose I'm *one of the symptoms of the times* . . ."

DIALOGUE WITH

R.D. LAING

A VERY ZANY, PECULIAR FIELD: SOME REACTIONS TO BASIC CONCEPTS

PART I

Overview | In this section Dr. Laing reacts to psychoanalysis and other basic concepts in psychology and questions the validity and effectiveness of certain trends. As we discuss Freudian theory, Dr. Laing suggests that Freud may have underestimated the earliness of childhood experiences. Exploring the theory of universal historical determinants brings out the difficulties encountered in universal constants of behavior and Dr. Laing offers interesting ethological parallels. We discuss Jung's constructs of archetypes and the collective unconscious, and he describes the qualifications required to develop a contemporary theory to explain the data that confront us. Finally, we discuss Jung's introvert/extrovert notion and the psychological mind games that often result from interpretations of this theory.

EVANS: Dr. Laing, although you've abandoned psychoanalysis in a formal sense, you were trained in psychoanalytical theory and involved in the psychoanalytic movement in your early years of practice. Looking at the field today, what do you still believe to be valid?

LAING: It's very difficult to say what psychoanalysis means today, since there are so many people who call themselves psychoanalysts, and practice so many different things under that name. I don't think there's one psychoanalyst who'd be prepared to recognize everyone else who calls himself that. When I was in analysis with Charles Rycroft at the London British Institute of Psychoanalysis, for instance, I wanted to be supervised by Melanie Klein. Protocol required that my analyst first check out the "lie of the land," and he reported back to me that Melanie Klein was unable to supervise me because she didn't consider *him* as properly analyzed. As far as she was concerned, I wasn't having the sort of basic experience in my own training analysis that would make it worthwhile for her to try to supervise me.

In another instance, I was told about an internationally known psychoanalyst who deviated considerably from Freud's position in a number of fundamental respects—in theoretical terms of the Oedipal complex, in timing of psychosexual development in infancy, and so on. His views continue to be "in" and have grown to be very influential. The senior analyst who told me about him said it was such a pity—when he was in analysis, a number of people knew his analyst to be developing a paranoid psychosis, but didn't feel they could tell him that! It's a very zany, peculiar field that we're talking about if we go beyond its public presentation. But I'm not terribly interested in doing this sort of thing at present.

EVANS: You are often perceived as having departed radically from psychoanalysis in your own thinking as well as in your therapeutic procedures. Perhaps we can be more specific. Take the notion of psychosexual development, or the idea that the individual is overdetermined by the combination of past biological and social events, in the sense of being influenced by the unconscious. Do these ideas continue to concern you and to be useful to you?

LAING: Oh, absolutely! More and more in my own experience of life—and in my sightings of other people's lives, as I move about the world, as I meet people in my practice, who come to me in distress—I become more deeply concerned. A person is confused, in a state of misery and consternation, with a helpless scattering of motor movement or postural behavior, and yet that person is not in any physical pain. He or she is examined by a doctor, all the tests are done, and there is nothing to account for his or her agony. Yet in Computersville this person is a nonfunctional biosocial unit. This state of affairs is picked up behaviorally. The disorder *manifests* itself to others in some aberration of behavior. But this same person might also be in even deeper distress without displaying obvious signs of distress at all. He could very well kill himself without ever raising his voice, without a scream, or even a whimper.

EVANS: Can you be a bit more specific about some of these ideas of Freud (1953) that have been of value to you?

LAING: In some way or another, very early experiences from *conception* influence all people significantly (I believe) but not *all* people in an obvious way, necessarily. There may be in some people—in some more than others—*obvious* effects in personality development, in the development of cognitive and emotional capacities and what Skinner (Evans, 1968) termed their application to life. Perhaps Freud didn't fully realize the earliness of those effects. Without diminishing anything that Freud said about later development, it seems plausible to me that the intrauterine experience, from conception, before implantation, and all the way to implantation, to birth and afterbirth experiences are mapped into our system in some way or another, and stored to express themselves later, especially surfacing after physical growth ends, and postpubertal adult life begins. One discovers as one gets older that the present situation, whatever it happens to be, doesn't entirely seem to account for one's present behavior. Any one individual's response to his or her present situation is not necessarily the response that everyone would have to that situation. Our response is a product of G (genetic system) and E (environment).

In our lives, professionally, personally, familywise, and in different stages of life—at fifteen, twenty-five, thirty-five, fifty, seventy—we are often so hard pressed that there's almost nothing we can do except fight for survival. We live often in states of polyvalence. Physical environmental factors, warmth, food, living accommodation, sleep, etc., may seem to be genetically expectable, yet the phenomenon of what is called neurosis and psychosis seems to be occurring. Generally speaking, in my life, my reaction to situations, my experiences, the emotional heights and depths and transformations I go through, seem to me to display a form and a syntax which I learned like language. I think there's a logic of the heart, a syntax common to every culture. We can't take any of the things that happen in our emotional lives out of the context of that structural field. This realm of discourse Freud explored. We must emphasize the social weave, the interrelatedness of psychic life, the interplay of our feelings, our ideas, our perceptions and experiences of the world within, the warp and woof of our life together.

EVANS: Would you say, then, that psychoanalysis has not done an adequate job of accounting for cultural effects on the individual, or the effects of the present? A theory of universal historical determinants is not sufficient to account for the entire behavior of the individual. Is this correct?

LAING: It's difficult to get down to what universal constants of behavior exist in any one species. Ethology presents the problem. The ethologist observes how animals actually behave in their own natural setting. He tries to classify behavior as it occurs in a genetically expectable environment, and to observe which aspects of that behavior appear to remain relatively constant or stable in different environments. Conduct is not only a specific set of movements, but a set of actions, with apparent ends in view toward which the actions are aimed. If we both move to lift a pen off this table, we could move on the left-hand tack or the right-hand tack. You might revolve in one direction, I might revolve in another. If we imagine ourselves studying behavior from a position suspended in distant "physical place," at that distance we look the size of ants on the face of the planet. From that degree of visual distance, human behavior appears as a swarming. We know nothing about the communication system or why they're doing anything, we just look at the shape of the thing they're doing. As Loren Eiseley says, it looks from that position as though the human species at present is a sort of congeries of spores, building capsules into spore-heap cities, crowding until they explode three feet out of the dung to another stuffed heap. Our perspective depends on whether we put ourselves on this planet or into space. I can entirely agree with the last chapter of Lévi-Strauss' *The Savage Mind* (1966), where he says that we cannot naïvely adopt any particular form of total world view or *Gestaltian* meaning our mind happens to find plausible. We can, however, place all these views—all of which display dramatic characteristics, reduced by Lévi-Strauss to diachronic transformations of binary elements—within the general framework of a world view.

EVANS: Your comments on Loren Eiseley bring to mind one of Carl Jung's (Evans, in press) most controversial constructs: the idea of archetypes and the whole notion of the so-called race or collective unconscious. As you know, Jung argues that in this collective unconscious reside the archetypes, quasi-Lamarckian, tradition-inherited symbols such as "the mother," "the father," "evil," etc. How do you feel about this line of thought?

LAING: I think it's one of the most fundamental

notions the human mind has come up with. It derives
from Plato and before in the West. Jung himself ac-
knowledged this, and not merely as a primitive culture's expression of more systematic and sophisticated
versions. The nature of possible and actual basic structural schematic forms that *in*form the human mind,
and find representation in images, has been considered
long before Jung. Descartes and Chomsky (1957,
1968) have evoked these matters, with Descartes' notion of language and Chomsky's congenial notion of
generative grammar. There is a generative unfolding,
along lines we can see, trace, and experience, which
we can discover, but which we cannot derive from any
more primitive, at present. Expressed through basic
schemata, experience presents itself to us, patterning
particular sets of redundancies we tend to take for
granted, and tend nowadays to construe as being either
environmentally and/or genetically programmed. The
data is incontrovertible. Everyone who studies the human mind comes up against the data to which such
theories point. How are we to account for that data?
Everyone who's faced with this data has to pause and
consider and ponder it. Lévi-Strauss' most fundamental theoretical position—both as expression of a
position and as influential generator—hasn't found its
way into the consciousness of psychologists in general,
and American psychologists, in particular, yet. God
help them when it does.

EVANS: But this idea of the collective unconscious,
the race unconscious of Jung, is considered controversial although it has really been presented from
Plato on by many writers. Are you saying that it's validated from your own observations?

LAING: Not quite. I said that the *seen* confronts the
seer. Jung presents more than observation. One of his

observations is that many people's minds are closed to the observations upon which his theories are based. There follow many abstract generalizations, influences, and assumptions—a certain amount of which isn't entirely clarified—that attempt to give the most acceptable, rational account of certain phenomena that we have before us in our own and other people's minds. One of the great points about Jung was that he was prepared to look at a lot of which very few people have been prepared to even begin to *imagine*. People turn away when they see the alchemical illustrations in Jung's books and say this is a lot of, you know, Cranksville. But all that is part of what the human mind gets manifestations of mental phenomena, as psychic realities, what the human mind makes and creates. Such productions of the human mind often appear to us grotesque and bizarre, in itself both scientific datum and analogy. Peculiar kinds of productions crop up again and again in the back wards of mental hospitals, in the world's museums, and in children's playrooms. People are always trying to make comparisons between dreams and the minds of nonindustrialized, nonurbanized contemporary cultures—psychosis, art, etc. Jung's theory attempts to put it together and say there are underlying structures traversing the board: universal processes at work, mental as well as physical-genetic. This field is up for grabs. It needs someone who can really develop it further. I haven't met an actual person imbued with the necessary combination of passion, intellect, psychological depth, and sensitivity to the data in which Jung enmeshed himself for years, and at the same time with the sophisticated information available that the first-level anthropologist demands: also stamina, and an untamed mind; not a mere addendum to the computer, but which appreciates the fundamental things. Somebody who has that combination might be able to bring before us a coherent contemporary account of psychosphere history. To my knowledge, this hasn't been done, but so much has been done that it could already have happened right around the corner to me, and I've missed it.

EVANS: You think, then, that Jung was a master theoretician who presented some challenging ideas that haven't been adequately integrated or even evaluated?

LAING: I don't think Jung was a *master* theoretician. He recalls us to our own minds: he gives us a theory, and a potpourri of assumptions, inferences, and generalizations, some, at one stage, of dubious political implications. We have a rich combination of things in Jung, including unavowed biases. Maybe I'm being less effusively enthusiastic than I might be. I regard Jung with great respect and I have studied him carefully over the years. He is undoubtedly a great psychologist.

EVANS: Aside from your obvious respect for a number of his theoretical constructs, what is there about Jungian theory or Jung's approach in general to which you take exception?

LAING: If we start at the beginning, he interpreted, at first mechanistically, his very interesting word association studies. Through what comes into view later as almost an "alchemistic" development of his early associationistic psychology, he developed the analogy of the "projective" personality test. I wouldn't take exception to what he was doing there. I suppose that right to the end of his life he was something of a mixture of simplistic scientific thinking and very sophisticated awareness of synchronic phenomena. I haven't got anything specifically against Jung. There's a claim that some of his work implies a racist ideology, and there's the tendency to centralize a "male" type, with the disposal of women to an "eternal" feminine type. The actual person—the man or woman—gets dissolved in a sort of spin-off into some inhuman universal. What does Jung, or Jungians, have to say about the *people* who are the crucibles in which these processes are occurring? Yet what Jung brings *in* makes me feel ungracious objecting to what he leaves out; for instance, what he leaves out in the way he approaches his psychology of alchemy. In his dream interpretations Jung dismisses as trivial much that Freud regarded as prerequisite to beginning to understand a dream. Jung disposed in too cavalier a manner the so-called personal repressed unconscious. At the same time he is right. There is a much vaster unconscious beyond that, much as a teacup compares to an ocean. There's an enormous and dynamically powerful collective unconscious manifesting basic patterns throughout the human species.

EVANS: Generally, the terms *collective* and *race* unconscious have been used interchangeably here, so that's what you mean, in the same sense.

LAING: Well, you used the word *race* and you said *species* unconscious.

EVANS: This is how it's often translated from the German. It's possible that Jung himself meant *species* rather than *race*. Jung, in the dialogue I had with him, was particularly troubled by the misunderstanding of his use of the terms *introvert* and *extrovert* as types of pathology. As you know, feeling, thinking, intuition, and sensation, coupled with extroversion and introversion, produced eight types that he meant simply as frames of reference. He was very concerned that people literally thought that individuals walking around were either introverts or extroverts. Jung wanted this type of approach used as a frame of reference to look at the organization of human personality. Does that make any sense to you, to think in terms of *introvertish* attitudes or *extrovertish* attitudes?

LAING: I suppose—without actually calling people introverts or extroverts—one of the ways in which we all think is in terms of whether we, or others, are turned inward or turned outward. These are terms that Freud used before Jung gave his particular amplified significance to them. Like many ideas and theories that exist in this field, for the most part I am sparing with them now because I've become more interested in actually looking at and directly experiencing the data itself, disposing of, for the moment, the concern to mark the data with constructs. Though we also need constructs—understood. This is a theory I particularly avoid because as a nondogmatic frame of reference it is brilliant and dangerous. It's so comprehensive, it covers everyone. It is also enormously fertile, so many ramifications. Introvert, extrovert; dominant, recessive; feeling, thinking; intuition, sensation; you can play with the combinations or permutations: consider the difference between men and women in those terms. You can consider the seesaw effect or the complementary effect in waking experience and in dreams, and so on. Someone can be an extroverted intuitionist in waking life and an introverted sensualist in dreams. The vistas that one can have playing a certain kind of mind game—scanning the data of one's experience in terms of that scheme and its elaborations—are endless.

THE CLASSIFICATION DILEMMA: WHAT IS "MENTAL"?

PART II

Overview | In this section Dr. Laing and I discuss the problems inherent in diagnosing and classifying disorders with behavioral manifestations. We trace the development of the organic-functional model, and Dr. Laing illustrates some of the limitations of this approach. He reacts to various historical and contemporary theories, including genetic, biochemical, geophysical, and environmental, and expresses the need for a total understanding of the overall situation—the politics of the situation—that will result in a theory underlying applied science that can be brought to bear helpfully on the individual in distress.

EVANS: Dr. Laing, perhaps the most widely noted observation made in your various writings has been your reaction to the whole matter of classifying mental disorders. Emil Kraepelin (1883) came up with a book of mental disorders that divided them into categories—neurosis, psychosis, the various subtypes —and the American Psychiatric Association periodically brings them up to date. They have become almost a bible to the traditional psychiatrist as he attempts to deal with his patients —to decide whether or not the patient will be hospitalized, for example, or how he can be treated. What exactly is your criticism of the classification of mental disorders? After all, we use diagnostic categories in the field of medicine, generally. Why should we be concerned about using diagnostic categories in the realm of mental illness?

LAING: I'm not saying that we should not use diagnostic categories as a matter of principle. We *do* use diagnostic categories, as you say, in the rest of medicine, in neurology and neuropsychiatry; in the rest of medicine, this is the procedure.

But in that vast domain of psychiatric practice—the so-called functional disorders—when persons are checked over completely and found, in the present state of our knowledge, to have nothing the matter with them *physically*, they are said to have something the matter with them *mentally*. This is a device, an extended metaphor, or analogy, that has become institutionalized and *politicized*. We have installations that are supposed to treat disorders of the "mind," dogmatically regarded as *due* to disorders of the body (at the molecular level, or the deeply programmed genetic level). It is part of what Ivan Illich (1975) has recently called the medicalization of *everything*, as a feature of our proliferating medico-industrial complex. Here it is the medicalization of mind. There are equally strong objections to the medicalization of the body. When we talk about having something or nothing the matter *physically*, we are often also in a zone of speculation, infinite cultural variation, and non-medical value judgments. We are hypothesizing that someone whose behavior and experience seem to be unaccountable by our usual categories may be suffering from something like schizophrenia, or some disease entity or syndrome. I don't even object to that, in principle, as a possibility. Sometimes I think it's very likely that we will discover—as with the extraordinary psychomotor changes with L-dopa—that something along this line may turn up for some people currently diagnosed as being psychotic.

EVANS: To help clarify this, let me be more specific. Admittedly, the term *functional* is very ambiguous, so let's go to the term *organic*, in the sense of organic psychosis. This seems to be an area in which the classifiers of mental disorders feel on firmest ground. Let's take a case such as alcoholic psychosis. Surely some of the neurologists believe that you can find real pathology or brain damage that causes this psychosis. Don't you agree?

LAING: That won't be easy to do. What's cause and effect? It has to be postmortem, doesn't it?

EVANS: Yes, and even that is not conclusive. So-called organic psychosis is not always that apparent.

LAING: Definitely not.

EVANS: What about psychosis due to aging—senile psychosis—where presumably you have arteriosclerotic disease?

LAING: As everyone who has been involved in geriatrics knows, it is difficult to draw more than tentative generalities from geriatric postmortems because you get this senile, demented person whose brain—preserved, sliced, and stained—shows microscopic changes, but you also find these changes in people who don't manifest the symptoms of senile psychosis.

EVANS: Perhaps some of our neurologist friends would grant that it might be difficult. Let's take another one, general paresis, or psychosis due to syphilis.

LAING: I'll give you an example of what is involved. This happened to an upper-middle-class Jewish family in Vienna before World War I—the world of Freud, *La Ronde*, and the great neurologist, who was studying general paresis of the insane. He was internationally known. My friend's mother, in her forties, began to have "nerves"—a very orthodox Jewish housewife could suffer from "nerves"—she was taken to the best specialist, naturally. He diagnosed her as suffering from syphilis. Just imagine what happened when the diagnosis of syphilis was bandied about in those circumstances! This is what was commonly done to the lives of thousands of people by that diagnosis, in those days. Freud was around the corner. You went to a proper neurologist though, if it was something to be taken seriously. If you were a woman, you were either a hysteric, or syphilitic, or something like that. If you were syphilitic, the "treatment" was malaria. You burned out the evil from their brains that way, since the torture and burning of witches was no longer "on." You set the system on fire with a malarial fever, then treated the malaria with quinine. She got the best treatment. I don't know whether it cured the GPI, but she died of the malaria. This possibility was explained at the beginning, of course, and understood by the family. The patient was subjected to a postmortem examination. His mother's body was cut up, disemboweled, "sectioned" into little bits, sliced up into smaller and smaller bits, put through all sorts of acid. And when they looked, no evidence of syphilis. Another misdiagnosis. It's in all the history books. How many doctors really regard that sort of thing as grotesque? This is the sort of thing that the specialist got a Nobel Prize for!

EVANS: I realize you're not suggesting that neurologists could never correctly see any type of organic pathology in some types of psychosis, but perhaps it would be a fairer inference, perhaps more important than whether or not there is some pathology, that there might be a heavy psychological loading in some of these disorders. In fact, maybe the psychological loading could be much more important than the pathology itself, even if it is found. Is that correct?

LAING: If I am disturbed, I may be disturbed spiritually, intellectually, emotionally, and physically. Many neurologists, once they find something, as they say "organic," they think that's it. The content of that heavy loading is of no interest. Even the notion that a

social system does have "organic" effects is remote to
many doctors. That there can be an interplay between
the spiritual, intellectual, emotional, physical, and the
social is even more remote to many. What a demean-
ing term—*emotional loading*. I find it very difficult to
discuss succinctly what I take to be the basic principles
of current opinion in these respects. When we come to
look at what this experience and behavior signify, we
have to consider that sometimes when a person comes
in with a black eye, sometimes that might actually
indicate that someone has punched their eye, and on
that simple basis, it's black. The extravasation of blood
into the soft tissue around the eyeball is certainly a
process genetically determined down to the last item.
In a genetically expectable environment, there is sudden pressure on the tissue; there is a response—a black
eye. There may have been no physical trauma, however.

EVANS: In discussing mental disorders in general,
you've said that even the so-called organic disorders,
symptoms of organic psychosis, are by no means as
cut-and-dried as we're led to believe. Moving into another realm, there are those who argue that there is no
such thing as a functional disorder in the sense that
functional means no final neurological basis, and that
ultimately we will find something biochemical going
on. Robert Heath (Heath, *et al.*, 1957, 1958, 1960,
1967) and his group at Tulane University in New Or-
leans have been working in this area for many years.
There are also those who feel that we're dealing with a
genetic phenomenon. The early work of Franz Kallmann (1953, 1958), for example, argues that schizophrenia is of genetic origin. Would you also have reservations about accepting a genetic or biochemical basis
for the so-called functional disorders?

LAING: I would have great reservations. In the first
place, I do not always regard those people, to whom
the diagnosis of functional disorder is applied, as necessarily having anything the matter with them. Suppose someone is placed in an environment set up to
disorder them. That is quite easy to do. Animals used
in ordinary laboratory experimentation have been de-
liberately driven crazy by environmental experimen-
talists, just to show how easy it is. We know that the
communicational environment alone can induce functional disorders and physical disorders. We know—at
least we ought to know—that there is nothing more
sensitive to social, psychological, communicational,
and environmental influence than the chemistry of the
body. The body chemistry is a contingency of unremit-
ting resonance with its social situation. Just think of
any emotion that accompanies a major shift in any
social position. Suppose, as Erving Goffman (1959)
showed, that we're suddenly demoted in social space.
A five-star general, wearing his five stars, is treated like
a private by a captain. I am sure we can all think of
examples from modern American history. Think of
what that must do, emotionally; without any great
stretch of the imagination, just think of what that
would suddenly do to his *chemistry*. Chemistry is
physical, organic. A catastrophic situation reverberates
through the adrenals, the pituitary, the lymphatics.
The whole endocrine system is brought into immediate, resonant play in any acute stressful social crisis.
All the neurophysiological chemistry stuff of the body
is a whole, implied in and by each of its components.
We are not some sort of genetically programmed arca-
num with no environment: a secret black box place
that responds only to internals.

It has been discovered that fields of energy on this

planet are extensions of the furthest blips picked up on the astronomer's telescope; the molecular structure of human cells vibrates in some way with the vibrations from outer stellar space. Our whole body is not primarily bounded by skin, but is part of a continuum of geophysical fields. Gay Luce's book, *Body Time* (1971), describes work on disturbed patients in Canadian mental hospitals in which they tried to find all the variables, including interpersonal ones—the staff going off and coming on, diet, medication, etc. They attempted to correlate these variables with sudden outbursts of violence observed in some of the patients and they couldn't find any correlations at all. When they fed the information to a space-research data-processing unit, they found exact correlations with certain geophysical storms, like sunspots, to which some people seem to respond more sensitively than others. Lunatics take their name from the moon. They are supposed to be people who are particularly sensitive to phases of the moon. We know the moon affects organic life and the phasing and maturation of organic processes. It affects all the waters of the earth. In the tides, an enormous amount of water moves up and down with the moon. Over eighty percent of our body is made up of water, and it seems inevitable that our fluids are going to be affected by such things as the moon. That's not Cranksville, that's perfectly ordinary common sense. The original Hippocratic practitioner, in the tradition of Western medicine, was expected to take into account the politics when he visited a place to treat a person. He ascertained what sort of social system existed, which way the winds blew, in many senses, what part of the year it was, and in the light of his sense of the social-cosmic context, he brought his focus to bear on the distress being felt by his patient. Until chemists and geneticists see the focus within the *context,* and realize there is an interplay between chemistry and social interaction, we can't develop the theoretical speculation at a pure science level we must have. Until we can, our so-called applied science is simply idiotic. I've gone over Kallmann's (1953, 1958)[1] work in detail and it is scientifically less than worthless. It's a disgrace. In fact, all the major published statistics so far, on monozygotic twins and twin family research, are, I would say, scientifically inconclusive, though some are great improvements on Kallmann. But not a single one of the major studies quoted in textbooks offers scientific evidence to confirm a so-called genetic theory of schizophrenia, nor do they "explain" even what they mean by "schizophrenia" . . . at least not to my satisfaction.

[1] See Appendix A for Dr. Laing's analysis of Kallmann's studies.

"SCHIZOPHRENIA"

PART III

Overview | Dr. Laing reacts to a classic definition of schizophrenia and suggests that psychiatrists may sometimes be as disordered as the patients they treat. He compares contemporary therapy to Inquisition techniques to illustrate what he considers to be a fundamental error in the set. Dr. Laing and I discuss the development of the double-bind family and he explains why he now considers this term too precise to describe the breakdown in communication that often immobilizes the "schizophrenic" member. To summarize this section, Dr. Laing presents brief case studies of two such families.

EVANS: You've said that you don't object to the classification of mental disorders, but you feel that many of the judgments implicit in these classifications are without any real foundation. In your own work and writing you have focused on a particular mental disorder, schizophrenia, which in the traditional classification, of course, is listed as one type of functional psychosis. Classically, schizophrenia has been described as a lacking in affect of the patient, the ultimate in withdrawal. It seems to be characterized by rather specific symptoms with different subtypes relating to paranoia, the basic regressive aspects of the disorder, and so on. To you, schizophrenia would be symptomatic of the limitations of such labeling. I gather you're particularly concerned because this is such a prevalent disorder, and because this label is so widely used. Is that correct?

LAING: Yes. It illustrates and epitomizes a certain sort of process which is widespread. To be a bit impish about it, we could say that it demonstrates a disorder, generally found all over society, to which some people are subject, many of whom have managed to reinforce their disorder in a socially acceptable way by becoming psychiatrists! They've institutionalized the disorder, which consists of being able to see in certain other people all the things they can't see in themselves. I would certainly think that people who are diagnosed as "schizophrenic" are often disorganized and disordered, but not in a way that is different from the way many psychiatrists are; who are, I would say in all seriousness, as disordered or more disordered than the patients they are diagnosing as disordered. A great degree of psychopathology and psychiatric theory is an institutionalized, reciprocally reinforced projection system applied by people to people, and that says, in many cases, more about the psychiatrist than it does about the patient. One reads more, for instance, about Kraepelin in his textbooks of psychiatry, to which you referred earlier, than about the people he's talking about. All you get is an endless verbiage of classificatory stuff represented as the epitome of the way the normal human mind should not work. Let me tell you about a lady I saw recently, typical of many, who felt she was going to scream. She had been tranquilized in the hospital for three months and still felt she was going to scream. No one had thought of letting her scream. If she could do it, why not? One of the big things about Janov (1970) is that he has actually managed to find a way to make screaming acceptable. Even though it's regarded as sort of dubious, people can actually scream. All right, we'll *let* people scream. It gets boring having all these people drunk and so on—we'll let them scream. We're doctors, though, and now there are a lot of people screaming. Our minds go gong! gong! gong! Classify! Pigeonhole! Do this and it's that classification, do that and it's this pigeonhole. We'll classify screams. There was an institution during the Inquisition a few hundred years ago—a very highly regarded group of men who were called prickers. They carried around pricks—needles of different calibers—that they used to stick through the skin and into the bone marrow of women who were thought to be witches. They listened to the screams. Did they scream or did they not? If they didn't scream, they were probably witches, able to counteract the exquisiteness of the pain. If they *did* scream, it had to be determined if the screaming was genuine or fake. This could be a witch who was inured to pain, who had taken some forbidden pain-killing drug and who was not really feeling the pain, just *pretending* to scream, in order to get off. So the prickers became experts, technologists, who could find the most painful part of the body, apply pain, and observe the reaction. It's the same sort of mind, the same sorry thing today. It's evil. I don't want to have anything to do with it. The whole thing ought to be dropped. It is a fundamental error in the original set, if you like, generating all these treatment programs and classifications, streamlining the classifications, then streamlining the treatments into more classifications, and on and on.

EVANS: It seems to me that you've used "schizophrenia"—I think I had better use quotation marks—as a test case for challenging the whole matter of classification. You developed this in a very intriguing manner in several of your books. As you learned more about it, you began to tie in the family as a particular factor. You seemed especially responsive to the work of Gregory Bateson (1956) who used the term *double-bind,* and you applied this term in a rather broad sense as you explored the family structure of the "schizophrenic." Now, at a relatively simple level, what do you mean by *double-bind,* as you use the phrase?

LAING: I use the phrase less frequently now, be-

cause in Bateson's sense, it's got a very precise meaning and I think there is something to be said for allowing that precision to remain. It should not be applied
to every situation where you might say you can't win
—on the spot, checkmated, stymied, tied in a knot.
Various internal and external systems playing off
against each other neutralize the command system so
that one can't move; one is immobilized, actually
brought to a standstill by the contradiction. Bateson
insisted on the nature of the paradox in this; that it's a
sheering strain or a dislocation between different type
levels, not straight head-on conflict between two sets
of the same type level. There are many different sorts
of contradictions, paradoxes, locks, binds, fangles, tan-
gles, impasses, check-and-checkmate situations for
which we haven't got a systematic language. We may
very well be developing one. I believe Bateson has begun this. In our environment we have these jams and
impasses of an interpersonal and social nature where
there's nothing physically the matter with the essential
processing capacities of an individual, but where the
person is exposed to such contradictory programs, injunctions, different types of data in different ways, that
the activating systems of the body "boggle," and one
gets into classifiable dysfunctional states.

EVANS: For that reason, it is evident to me why you
don't use the term as much as you once did, but recall-
ing your focus on what you call the "double-bind family" in the background of the "schizophrenic," can you
specifically describe what the situation would be like
for that member who is the victim of such a family?

LAING: A diet of unavowed lies seems to me more
difficult to take for some people than others—a genetic
variable, no doubt. Some seem not to mind, even to get
"off" on it. Let's say the quotient of truth and decep-

tion in a communicational system varies. There may be no *meta*-communicational system which recognizes this fact; the meta system may be consonant with the deceptive *alpha* systems, so the *beta* and other *meta* systems comment paralinguistically—at times actually linguistically—on the linguistic *alpha* system. This may be denied. Any questioning of the truth/value propositions displayed in the *alpha* systems may be punished. I can think, right off, of several cases where I have been presented with a member of a family—mother, father, son, or daughter—not sure who they were, and agonized by consternation and bewilderment as to what was true and what was not true. The family tries to be sympathetic, to help. They say they want to do the best thing. They say that money is no object. They also say that they doubt this person's sanity. Chemical treatment hasn't "worked." No treatment has "worked." They come to me and decide they have to level with me. The mother tells me, "You know, my husband's not really his father. I never told him that. He does everything for that boy, but they never got on together. He's not like my eldest daughter. She takes after her dad, but he's never seemed to take any interest in her." And so, in an extraordinarily naïve way, they come out with something in the past which might very well cause anyone in that situation to pick up cues of such confusion, such dishonesty and duplicity, about his or her identity, as to find oneself in a state of bewilderment, with no idea why. Try to ferret it out. "I don't feel like you're my father." "How could you possibly say that?" This is a gross example. Many of my examples are gross. But sometimes it's much more subtle.

EVANS: And of course you're relating this to some later disturbance in the person. You don't like the label, "schizophrenia," but would you go so far as to

say that there are greater or lesser degrees of this dou-
ble-bindedness in most families in our society?

LAING: It depends more or less on how tight the
tuner key is turned, and what calls for it. After being
involved for a number of years in the study of families
where at least one member was diagnosed as schizophrenic, I did some studies with Esterson and some
other people of "normal" families to provide ourselves
a contrast. This work hasn't been published. We looked
at these families, ordinary families in London, in the
same way we looked at the families of the people diagnosed as schizophrenic. We ran into major methodological difficulties in making comparisons between
group processes. I didn't have the mathematics of
groups—quite advanced mathematics—to resolve these
problems. So for that and other reasons, we have not
yet published this research. It's difficult to describe
adequately the sort of comparative data we got, but I
can give you an example of where the similarities and
the differences lie.

One family had two daughters. One was a sixteen-
year-old girl who worked in a bank. She had been cry-
ing and vomiting the day before we met the family in
their home for the first time, but she had recovered and
was feeling better by the time we arrived. A problem
had developed over the fact that she went around with
a pop group and had started to pair off with one of the
boys in it. Her mother had taken her aside and explained to her that it was bad for the morale of the
group to develop such a one-to-one relationship, and
for that reason she should give it up. No one in the
group had asked the mother to do this. The daughter
had been upset, had lost a day's work, vomited, been
off her food, and then had perked up and now said
how grateful she was to her mother who could give her

such very sage advice. She didn't fight it. She gave the boy up. She continues to work at the bank and maintains her relationship with the other boys in the group. Now she's told by her father, in front of us, "Of course, she's very romantic—she's like my elder sister who never got married. On Saturday afternoon you could see her down in the main street with this boy, looking at bedroom wallpaper." This girl is told she's very romantic, *but*. It's complicated. Clearly that is not the beginning or the end of it. In this instance, except for the transitory "disorder" of vomiting, being off her food, and taking to her bed for a day, she is able to continue to be "normal," to go back to work in the bank. Suppose, though, that she couldn't give the boy up. Suppose it continued to gnaw at her. Her father and mother and sister are enjoying thinking of everyone else's good, but a ferocious struggle begins to develop. What is this girl going to do? She's "romantic," like her aunt who never married. When there's a knock on the door, what is she going to do? I think the same thing could develop in that family that has developed in the past in other families regarded as "schizophrenogenic."

A FANTASTIC DIVIDING LINE: THE PROFESSIONAL ROLE TODAY

PART IV

Overview | In this section Dr. Laing and I discuss both the training and the professional role of the mental-health specialist, including the economics of the institutions that provide the training and establish the roles. He describes the evolution of a contemporary model based on the exigencies of World War II that has been carried over into civilian life. Dr. Laing suggests that professional training may actually culture out the ability to communicate, and he calls for a reconsideration of priorities that will lead to more open relationships. In conclusion, we discuss alternative methods of training, research, and therapy that maintain the precision of science yet respect the needs of the human beings involved.

EVANS: Dr. Laing, a question occurs to me that would be of great interest, not only to psychology students, but to the faculty members of medical schools and graduate programs in psychology and social work. This concerns how to train individuals in the mental-health specialties—psychiatrists, social workers, psychologists, clinical psychologists. To some degree, as you know, we've gotten hemmed in by a certain style of training. There has been a trend, a kind of movement—the community psychology or social psychiatry movement—that seems to take the focus of training away from the traditional face-to-face situation and out into the community. I'm sure that you have developed some ideas about how we might do a better job.

LAING: I appreciate the difficulties of everyone in this field, including my own, where we work within different institutional and organizational frameworks which are funded in different ways. The institutional economics of the professional life seem to be one of the most important areas that we ought to take stock of, on several counts.

This has been pointed out recently by a number of people, and I think more people are going to be looking at this and, hopefully, developing alternatives. Once you have the backing of a professional stance by massive economic interests, then both theory and practice in that profession are in danger of serving the ends of the economic interests that are paying for it (Illich, 1975). This is a very difficult area because the professionals are being paid to do a job with money that is coming ultimately from the people, mainly in the form of taxes, but it comes in such a roundabout way. These welfare programs are developed from somewhere *else,* and they have great difficulty delivering the product or commodity to the people who are supposed to be the beneficiaries. In the mental-health field what is *supposed* to be bought, to a great extent, is not a manufactured commodity that can be handled, or even *mere* technique, but a capacity to be openheartedly available to other people. You might say that this puts the psychiatric, the psychoanalytic, the psychological, the social work, and related professions in a position that is fairly analogous to that of prostitution, at its best. What is being paid for is *relationship.* You are training people to have as their specialty, their marketable commodity when it comes to the bit, the capacity to bring themselves—their bodies, minds, and sensibilities—into relationship with people in situations which are beyond the range of ordinary common sense in our culture. This tends to develop an elitism that reinforces the diffidence of the ordinary nonspecialist person's confidence in his or her own capacity to understand. All over the place individuals and clusters of individuals get so knotted up, so screwed up, so embroiled in very complex situations that no one in the situation knows what is going on. Someone must be brought in to intervene in the hope that intervention will in one way or another bring some clarity to the situation, so that the confusion of the people will be mitigated in some way.

EVANS: You're saying that the economic interests in our society that support medical, psychological, social work training—the university structure—are more or less dedicated to an already existing system and that those economic interests build certain limitations into what can go into this training. Suppose you were the dean of a medical school, or the chairman of a psychiatry department, or the director of a social work program (which doesn't seem very likely), but suppose you had an ideal situation. What things would you put into the curriculum to increase the probability that the students would develop or grow into this openness toward people that you obviously consider so important?

LAING: Before I try to approach that very important question, let me say that I am not putting forward, in what I said before, anything like a blanket condemnation of the system or just saying the easy thing—that the system is entirely self-serving, or the individuals that comprise it are self-serving. Our interdigitated plurality of systems is the product of the individuals who compose it, so I am not talking about the system itself as some entirely alien, malevolent, paranoid-persecution-machine structure that is devouring everyone in it, though some of us no doubt sometimes feel that way. If I were the dean of a medical school, or holding any position of that sort, I couldn't just change the curriculum quite like that. When it comes to the nitty-gritty of anyone's particular job, I am not in a position to tell him how he should act better or say, "Here is what you should do." I can talk about certain considerations and certain matters of principle and certain specific matters of practice. One of my earliest encounters with institutional psychiatry was as a psychiatrist in the British Army at the time, not long after World War II, when British and American psychiatry had been raised to the dignity of a full-time speciality. There were a number of senior psychiatrists, like Menninger, who felt that psychiatry had been oversold in the army. Now what helped to oversell it was such things as a paper by a British psychiatrist called "The Economic Use of Manpower in the British Army."[1] The point of this paper—just plain common sense—was that an army will not get its tanks fueled and driven efficiently, won't get its airplanes going, or anything like that, if you have lots of square pegs in round holes. He said that in a military system you need men who "fit" into this niche or that, and who, if they are doing what they want to do and can do well, will work better, and the machines will be better served. Therefore, the army should employ certain people to run this side of the show—human engineers. And the best people for that job were people with medical training, physicians who "specialized" in disturbances of behavior. This has become much more sophisticated than it was thirty years ago. This sort of thing, hopefully, would serve the interests of all parties, although all interests might not be entirely coincident when it comes to any one single guy who might want out, unconditionally. There might be a lot of people who want to be out that the army wants to be in, and when it comes to such an issue, it is very much a matter of what mood one happens to be in as to how one will inflect the balance of contending interests. If someone wants out, for instance, it is very easy just to say that

[1] Professor Ronald Hargreaves, later professor at Leeds University.

he is emotionally malfunctioning—a personality dis-order, an inadequate personality, psychopathic, etc. If you really want him out completely, and if he wants to take the stigma of being a homosexual, a schizoid personality, or even psychotic, then he'll be out, probably. But he will be picked up by the com-puter for life. That is already part of it, you know, all such data are beginning to be programmed into the world-computer-brain. That's one extreme of a system that psychiatrists are part of, and there are quite a lot of psychiatrists who have been among the architects and designers of this system. That's a growing side of life that's far from the consciousness of many people. In a way I haven't got anything to say about it, except that I hate it. I saw that that wasn't where my contribu-tion could lie. At the time I felt more desperately and unreconciledly negative about the development of the whole thing but I now feel that it has already devel-oped into such a worldwide network, expressing and accommodating to a new socioeconomic reality, that, without detesting it less, I see no way to turn the clock back. I don't see what can be done about it, without human beings refusing to treat human beings in that sort of way.

EVANS: Let's take this one extreme you're talking about. You're saying that the model we saw during World War II was really the first time that psychiatric and psychological input played such a powerful role with so many people concerned. You say that such a scale—

LAING: —got into the governments, industry, the military, into the way the whole system now works.

EVANS: And this model, in a sense, was carried over into civilian programs after the war? And thus became a model that you say is a response to a need somehow to place people, as you put it, square pegs in square holes. Now you say that since you can't turn the clock back, you cannot fault it. You used the term *prostitution,* earlier. Are you using this to describe the people who are trained to fit into the system? I don't think you are necessarily saying that every psychiatrist or psychologist or social worker who becomes part of this system, responding to immediate needs in hospitals or institutions or even in clinical practice, is a prostitute. You're really saying that they are caught up in the system, aren't you?

LAING: Oh, I'm not putting down the profession of prostitution, and least of all, psychiatry. I'm glad that it hasn't been more explicitly and formally institutionalized. It is still a free-lancing activity. I mean that quite seriously. I remember that Donald Winnicott— who used to be president of the International Psychoanalytical Society, and who was one of my teachers— used to be fond of making, in all seriousness, the comparison between himself as psychoanalyst and the prostitute. He felt that a prostitute is someone who makes himself or herself available—"to stand in for," as the word literally means—to stand in for someone else's fantasy, physically, emotionally . . . The prostitute in a physical sense (and not only physically, often) becomes the person who stands in for the needs of the client as the psychiatrist stands in for the needs of the client. The method differs. Although the method of dealing with this "transference" on the part of the psychoanalyst is considerably different from that of the prostitute, there is a certain comparison.

EVANS: Just a few years ago the American Psychological Association had a serious symposium on the ethics and responsibilities of the clinical psychologist or mental-health worker, with respect to getting sexually involved with patients.

LAING: An official Japanese psychiatrist calls the client's courtesan or whatnot "adjunctive therapy," and they do the same thing in Sweden. It may very well be a spreading practice. It contravenes the Hippocratic oath, however.

EVANS: In other words, the circle is actually closing, finally! Getting back to the question of training, a good deal of what is going on in training in psychology, social work, and psychiatry programs is designed to equip individuals to fit into this system, which meets a need—in a sense, as you say, as a prostitute.

LAING: And as an administrator and as someone who can contribute to making the system work. I'm not saying whether or not I would like to see the system working better, I am just saying that it is a fact of life that some people seem to shy away from and get embarrassed and defensive about. It is very difficult to have an ordinary conversation with some people about this consideration because so much special pleading comes in. That's one side. But what is being paid for in those branches of the psychiatric thing has to do with the actual encounter meeting—person-to-person, face-to-face—with people who are called patients. For whatever reason, for someone's "good," or because he or she has become insufferable to those they live with, complete strangers are now being moved into the house by other people. A child is taken away from its mother, the mother is stripped of her legal "rights," may not be allowed "out," may not be allowed to see her child. She has no money. A father is taken away, and whether he wants it or not, he is going to get severe things done to him inside his skin, which will change his mind, his chemistry, his body. Electricity is going to be shot through his brain whether he wants it or not—very often when he doesn't want it. There are a tremendous number of medical-legal issues there. But some people are on to the abuses of lobotomies, for example. The women's liberation movement is aware that three women are being lobotomized to each man. A distinguished American neurosurgeon—you don't have to wait for the Soviets to produce this—suggested that lobotomy a number of years ago might have been the answer to the "Communist menace." You don't have to lock up subversive dangerous political people. Lobotomize them. Better, split their brains. I think these things are dreadful. They reinforce persecution by more persecution. There is an "operation" for almost anything, even death. But we haven't gotten to the thing that I'm particularly interested in: that there is still a domain, an arena in which one human being actually gets into the same place at the same time to meet another human being. This is what all this infra- and superstructure should be for: to allow somebody to meet somebody, or even several people. It seems to me that the medical student in this country and in America has been trained to be competent, to receive input, to keep it unscrambled, and to reproduce it as output in the form of a written communication, or in terms of well-organized, syntactical, correct answers to questions in oral examinations. They must be able to examine patients in a clinical setting, make informed judgments, and then be able to express those judgments in a formal manner, in the form of an oral examination. These are the skills a medical student has to develop to pass his exams and qualify. After he has qualified in these preliminary examinations, he still has several more years of "advanced" training before he is fully postgraduately qualified for the upper echelons of the profession. In the course of that time he is going to be very lucky, within the context of his professional life, if he hasn't had *cultured out* of him his capacity to relate to other people in a personal way, even within the framework of his professional role. I don't see that being a professional need necessarily preclude someone's being able to be openhearted and open-minded, but it seems to happen to many people. This, of course, is a story that has been taken up by a number of other people and I hope that it will be amplified. If the effect or the implication of all that training, all that money, all that planning and organization is in the service of facilitating arrangements for people to come together with people without fear—so that the ground can be cleared, so that an open space is created, so that communication can occur—then it is all to the good. What about the apprenticeship method? Suppose you were going to institutionalize the practice of painting. Industry and governments are now going to pay people to paint and there will be diplomas and "degrees" and licenses. Anyone without some recognized bit of paper will not be allowed to paint. There will be, however, some people who are painters, who will continue to paint. And it will be forgotten that the only way, or the best way, that anyone can learn to paint is to apprentice himself, to hang around as an apprentice to someone who is actually painting. Now that doesn't mean that one can learn to pass exams in painting, or talk about it fluently, or even be good at the administration that is behind it. It means that one can actually paint. In talking about this, of course, all the words can sound perfectly well, and still come out of the mouth of a complete idiot. It is not the content of the words, but something that we find greatly difficult even to put into words. As Whitehorn demonstrated in a series of experiments, different psychiatrists at different ages, with different personality structures that are measurable, seem to be able to get into different relationships

with people. Some hit it off better than others. When
that personal relationship does click, it is the single
most important therapeutic factor in the whole thing.
Someone who is in a state of consternation, bewilderment, confusion, or terror can settle down and become
much less frightened, can breathe more freely. The
fear that is producing the mental scatter can diminish
in just the presence of another human being on the
same wavelength, not putting over any numbers, who
is not doing anything to evoke reinforcement of the
anxiety thing. Even though it doesn't last, in five or ten
minutes the effect of an actual person in relationship
to a frightened person is of more measurable influence
—cutting out, eliminating ninety percent of the psychopathological behavior of someone in this disturbed
state—than any other procedure I have heard of. Now
if, in our training, we only tell people how to use
drugs, how to push buttons, how to be instrumentally
effective in doing this, that, and the next thing, we lose
the substance in the pursuit of shadows. We lose the
baby, I feel, with all this attention to the bath water.
If the people who are in charge of training, the dean
and his faculty, are alert to this in whatever circumstances they find it, their minds will dictate the laying
down of a practice that will be, under the circumstances, the best that one can find. They can then pro-
ceed upon those principles in the light of that understanding.

EVANS: What you are describing, what you are
talking about, is the therapeutic personality. You're
suggesting that Whitehorn's experiment demonstrated
that, in the right combination of circumstances, the
therapist will be very, very effective. You're almost implying something that transcends formal training and
treatment. You're familiar, of course, with the widely

discussed Bethesda study in which a group of sympathetic housewives was trained and involved in carrying out therapeutic activities. With the "right" type of personality, they were able to do a very effective job. In a sense, you may be talking about something that is unrelated to formal psychiatric or psychological training. You're talking about something that is fairly intangible in the sense that a person can't be trained to have this particular quality. If Whitehorn had used a control group of people who were not psychiatrists at all, or professionally trained therapists, who were just compassionate people, he might have had the same results with respect to certain types of—

LAING: He might have had better results. My impression, derived from participant observation, from students who approach me about this, and from older, senior people in this set of professions, is that the present professional training may actually be culturing out the aptitudes that we want to draw out and cultivate. Education (in one of its edifying etymological senses) means educing, drawing out, the capacity—the native flair, if you like—that some people have. This can be educed, or drawn out of someone. Now you can draw that out of a housewife, you can even draw it out of a medical student. You can allow it to flower. It has nothing to do with the capacity to take in from a written print-out some sort of information, process it, and then bring it out again. Turning one's mind over to being a biocomputer—a rather inefficient adjunct to the world computer that is developing—is not the sort of thing that I would consider to be in the domain of such aptitude. It is not the kind of thing I would like to see develop as the distinctive competence in this field. The fact that one has gone through all that means that one has got oneself into a position in the power elite. By showing that one can do that, one is accepted into the side of the system that is on the side of the desk from which the program is set up. They are the people inside the building, who planned the building, and who are now in it. But there's the whole world of people who are on the outside of the building. They are often the children, the families, the friends, and relations of the people who are on the other side of the desk. There is a fantastic dividing line there, and there doesn't seem to be any way that it can be got over. But the people who are in the professional role certainly shouldn't think, in finding themselves in that position in social space, that they have acquired any claim to distinctive competence that a housewife—given the chance to spend time with disturbed people—has not possibly got to a greater degree.

EVANS: Looking at this from a slightly different point of view, and I think your own work has contributed to this, one of the most frequent statements made by research psychiatrists and psychologists in this field is that we have a criterion problem. Perhaps doing a good job doesn't necessarily require a trained psychiatrist, or psychologist or social worker. Perhaps a housewife, with a certain "feel" for people could alleviate psychopathology. Now the criterion problem always seems to bring up what is meant by alleviating, what, in fact, is meant by psychopathology? If we accept this openness that you describe, this ability to relieve the individual, this capacity that has nothing to do with training, then we are almost going to have to define, in very precise detail, what this capacity amounts to. Certainly it doesn't mean allowing the patient just to go away feeling better for the moment. What are we talking about? What does it really mean? If we say that there are people who have this certain special compassion, what does it amount to? What are we producing through this transaction, through this type of therapy? It is, of course, almost impossible actually to know the effects of therapy. You certainly have heard that question raised many times. If we are going to say that X can do a good job doing therapy, the next question almost certainly is "What is therapy?" or "What are you trying to produce with this process?"

LAING: As I said at the beginning, there seems to be a fundamental paradox in a system that has come to think entirely in terms of production. There is the production of things, objects, matter derived from material and assembled in a certain way, produced in the form of something that can be handled, that becomes a commodity. There is a price on it; it can be bought and sold. All these programs of community therapy, all these things that are being done under that general set of activities, are thought of, almost exclusively, in terms of production of a commodity—results. Although you can't see it, touch it, or feel it, therapy has now become a commodity. It's an elitist practice with a market value. There is a type of mentality with the bit between its teeth, now searching around to find the commodity that has been paid for. It's very elusive. It might be that there is an error in some premise. We may be looking for a nonexistent product, because if there is a "result," what is it? There is a relationship that you can't measure. You can put the sound on tape and do a whats, wheres, and whens count. You can do a formal analysis; you can do a more or less sophisticated linguistic, paralinguistic, kinetic analysis. You can produce more and more mathematically sophisticated and sharper indices of "autism," or its opposite, for example. One can get into hand movements, finger movements that can be judged in terms of the rate of change from rest to certain movements that stop suddenly as other movements take over. OK. None of those things seems to be particularly convincing to me and they are not particularly convincing to the people who do them either, often because, I think, we must consider what we are trying to measure, what we are trying to control or manipulate, what we're trying to buy and sell, what results we want, given our environment and genes. What is the product? What is the domain in which this particular transaction is occurring? Let's take feelings, emotions, affects. In an ordinary, good enough, genetically expectable environment we would not especially obscure the subject. We're dealing with how people feel. Let's take feelings such as anger, pity, tenderness, love, jealousy. These are not in the domain of touchable objects. I defy anyone to lay out jealousy for me to see. By certain criteria of behavior, perhaps you can distinguish a jealous person, but even that is not easy to do. It's really an inference theory.

EVANS: That's all you can ever do. You can never do more than infer something that may be called jealousy. There is no other way to get at it.

LAING: Yes. Jealousy, et cetera, can "scientifically" be inferred, although it may be directly experienced, like all these human emotions that are not the subject matter of direct "scientific" study. We've got a sort of thinking going on now which argues that if we can't support an experience with the "hard" data of science, the experience doesn't count. It is discounted. The hard data of science are sight, touch, taste, smell, objects, but these, to science, merely give indications of states of affairs that are extra- or para- or metasensory. The recent advances of science have gone through the apparent manipulation of a domain of energy we cannot see, touch, or taste, or smell directly. The scientist has to come back to his observations however, to the things he *can* see and hear and touch and taste and smell. We're all living within that phenomenal framework and we infer (within the scientific rules) what is going on outside it.

But there is a special problem about *feelings*. On the one hand, they are more directly immediate than anything else, and on the other, they are scientifically so remote that many scientists hardly regard them as existing.

The principle of not multiplying hypotheses unnecessarily seems excellent, but there is a strange tendency to turn this into the proposition that what science does not know how to study does not exist. This is to deny reality, because we haven't an hypothesis to account for it. In that case, we might as well say that nothing exists, and quite a few people have said that.

It's not just turning one's skin inside out, trying to look "objectively" (from outside) at what is "subjective" (inside)—an incredibly alienating procedure. We have not even the precise proper word for it. Merleau-Ponty writes of structure of behavior and the primacy of perception, trying to reveal a radical transformation, currently going on in the human experience of space and time and all their elements. Something is happening to the way the human environment is actually experienced by human beings that releases and facilitates—in fact, dictates—a type of practice that wouldn't arise unless one's environment was experienced in that manner. Certain things wouldn't even begin to occur to one as relevant or meaningful, or even *as* a human activity, unless one was seeing the world in a particular way. And some people seem to find the world, seen this particular way, annihilating to them, persecuting to them, destructive to them, in terms of their feelings, in terms of what it feels like to be a human being. If *we* are looked at in this way—as often represented in *Scientific American* models—you can't distinguish on paper where the flesh begins and the instruments end. It's all the same. But if one feels one is a machine, a robot, a device, not hung together in terms of organic unity, that's regarded as a state of schizoid, psychopathological deterioration, depersonalization, and whatnot. That very mentality, when it crops up in certain manifestations, is considered to be almost the epitome of psychopathology. But it's actually to be found in its most rampant, pure form when it crops up in another sort of manifestation—in the minds of the people who *are*, generically, this very psychopathological theory they are propounding. The very psychopathology that is being studied is demonstrated most clearly by the people who are creating the psychopathological theory. If you want to see it and read about it, if you want a perfect example of schizophrenia, just read a psychiatric text like Bleuler's (1951) textbook on schizophrenia or any of Kraepelin, especially his case histories, or any number of more recent things, and you will see manifested in the mentality of the psychiatrist the very disease, the very psychopathology, that is projected onto the person who is supposed to be the patient. I would say that the fallacy, the switch around, the confusion—I don't feel that I have found a way to give adequate articulation to this, but I'm trying—is a profound crisis of a shifting transformation as we move through this rapid, transient phase of whatever it is we are doing to ourselves and to the world. Or being done to.

EVANS: Coming back to the problem, let me pull together what we are discussing here. You're arguing

that institutionalized psychology, psychiatry, and social work are responding to needs in the same sense
that they responded to needs during World War II,
and are continuing to train people who can go out and
offer their services, almost like prostitution, in the sense
that society considers these services a necessary evil—
a commodity—and as such, reluctantly tolerates them.
You, of course, are offering an alternative view. You're
arguing that the whole system is based on faulty assumptions to some degree. In training students, should
we first try to acquaint them with the state of the art
and then move them away gradually as we change the
training, so that we develop a new breed no longer
trapped into the present system? Or should we maintain this system and gradually erode its effect? Do you
think these are probabilities?

LAING: It's in the interest of all of us to make *our*
system work for *us*. It has become *our* world. This is
completely political, one might say, and also completely nonpolitical. The top brass are as desperately
alienated in and by the system they may think they
control as the dustmen, who also sometimes develop
delusions of grandeur. Every human being has an interest in making this system work on behalf of life on
this planet, women, men, the young and old, the birds
and animals and plants. We want it to work on our behalf. *They* are all *us*. We want all this hardware we've
got, all this stuff that we're producing and exchanging,
all the money and all the things that money can buy, to
be serving or servicing *us*. But it's a very tricky position, very ambiguous, and when we look at it in some
ways, we are already rather inefficient machines serving machines of our devising, upon whom we have become abjectly dependent. We've got to service the
machines that service our lives. We can get machines

to service machines and then we've got to service those machines. We've got a system in which we're being devoured by our own shit. It's using us up, and using our children up. That nightmare has already been articulated by others in some detail. It must be grasped more. Psychiatry and social psychology, sociology, anthropology—all the human sciences—are at the very heart of the dilemma. These disciplines study human beings in their ecosystems (Bateson, 1972). They have to do with the relationships between human beings themselves. But we all now know that these relationships are in a *context*. What we've got to keep in mind, it seems to me, is that, in academia, whether it's medical school, in the training of an anthropologist, or a social psychologist, the training must attempt in theory and in practice to clear away the rubble, to clear some ground, so that some relationships between some people can exist, even temporarily, where and when it is possible to breathe a little more freely— sanctuary, asylum, where life-in-relation can flower. Is that now a utopian dream? The field of competence of these distinctive *human* sciences isn't as naïvely confined to human beings alone as most theories and practices in psychology, et cetera, give students the impression, because our "human" environment is largely a nonhuman environment. Relationships between human beings occur within a context of the physical, nonhuman environment, a great deal of which is now human artifact. We can't put the clock back—this is the field in which we're operating. If we keep ourselves as clear as possible about it, if we orientate our theory to keep the central point, if we use the machines to facilitate getting together instead of being shredded apart in the service of the machines, if we don't turn ourselves into machines and don't treat other people as machines, and if we don't allow ourselves to be treated as machines, we still may not finally end up with machines servicing machines, as the nearest we can glimpse of what the savage minds of our grandfathers once called love, charity, and compassion.

"Take good care of your wife," an M.D. once said to me, as a fellow doctor, "she's your most important piece of equipment."

IN A SOLITARY WAY WE ARE ALL BYSTANDERS

PART V

What Is a Bystander?—Crime/
Cambodia/Concentration
Camps | When Paranoia
Comes True: Nazi Suspicion and
Jewish Apathy | You Never
Think of Telling the Truth—
Watergate and More | A
Five-Channel Synchronized
Hallucination:ESP/Mind
Control/Some Far-Out Re-
search | The Tip of the Ice-
berg: A Very Basic Human
Condition

Overview | Dr. Laing reacts to current research in the area of bystander apathy, generalizing to such broader issues as the seeming apathy of the Jewish people in the face of Nazi extermination during World War II, and the more recent situation in Southeast Asia. We discuss Watergate and the worldwide political implications of truth-telling, communication, and control. Dr. Laing suggests that in the future more barbaric methods may be replaced by subtle, but equally effective, forms of mind control generated by contemporary research being carried on around the world. We conclude this section with some comments on the basic nature of the human condition that can lead to such problems, individually and nationally.

EVANS: You made a point earlier, about interest in our fellowman, saying that living in the kind of barren system that you described, we should all be cultivating this interest much as we do flowers or plants. As a social psychologist I am particularly aware of a line of research that appears rather conflicting, triggered off by the Kitty Genovese case in Queens, New York. As you know, a group of onlookers stood by and allowed an individual to be attacked violently, without lifting a finger to help. This has led to a tremendous interest in what we call bystander apathy, and in turn, to the whole area of altruism. There are those who argue, making sweeping generalizations from such happenings, that this type of incident is an indication of the increasing indifference of man to his fellowman, that it shows how morality and concern are falling to pieces. Subsequent research into this matter, however, doesn't come up with that clear-cut a picture. It seems to show that there are conditions under which people will help and conditions under which they will not. In terms of your previous state-

ments, how do you feel about these observations of bystander apathy? Are they symptomatic of the lack of
interest you've described, or do you feel that the whole
thing has been overstated? I'd like to have your feelings here, your hunches. I know you haven't specifically studied this area.

LAING: I haven't had much direct relevant experience with this. For instance, I've never seen that happen myself. I've never found myself in the position of
having to choose whether I'm going to be a bystander
who will walk on, literally, or stand by, or get into a
real heavy punch-out which might mean being per-
manently damaged physically, or killed. And the
chance might be remote that by such action one would
indeed be able to help, one might be just another victim. That's an agonizing decision. Before we start talking about bystander apathy as a feature of the aliena-
tion of vast urban population complexes and all that,
consider that we don't know much about bystander
apathy fifty years ago or a hundred years ago. I imagine there was plenty of it. People have always been
frightened. What is a bystander? There is now only the
chorus, I think Ortega y Gasset remarks somewhere.
What about bystander apathy concerning Cambodia?
It's absolutely ridiculous to say that no one knew about
Cambodia, because the military kept double-book-
keeping. Everyone who was interested in knowing
knew, that in the sixties, the military struggle in Indo-
china was far more extensive than was being let on.
Cambodia was being bombed. God knows what else is
going on there now. Look at the German bystander
apathy about the concentration camps. Look at the
British apathy when their bomber command destroyed
a city like Dresden, just to show the Americans and
Russians what the British Air Force could do. What

about the bystander apathy that we know of everywhere? I'm not convinced I'm holier than anyone else; when it comes to the bit, I'm not sure that I'm not a bystander, whether or not I'm apathetic. Whether we're pathetic or apathetic, we are all, millions and millions of bystanders.

EVANS: You bring up the greater issues. It may not be just a question of the Kitty Genovese case, but something much more basic, such as the way we stood by and watched the Nazi atrocities develop, as you pointed out. But to follow up a point we discussed earlier, what about this curious case that several playwrights and authors have explored, this strange apathy of the Jewish people themselves as they were led into these camps to be exterminated? They just seemed to stand by and let it happen. Does that seem to be a curious situation to you? Surely they could have pooled their resources under those conditions, or at least struggled rather than just being led in.

LAING: From the reports of the survivors of those camps, as you know, one of the most prominent things seemed to be that so many couldn't believe it was happening. I mean, in Germany, in many an ordinary German town, Jews were not seemingly isolate. They were Europeans like everyone else, in a "civilized" town, living in a "civilized" manner. The Nazis were at the time, apparently, their neighbors, people they went to school with, shopped with, worked with, played with. Very difficult, actually, to *realize* that what was happening was actually happening. Just like now, say, if the English decided to round up all the Scots in a very highly bureaucratically planned operation, unreported in any of the media. You open the door and quite politely, sometimes, they tell you to come along. They wait for you to get dressed, quite politely, and then off you are taken to become margarine. You're going to be processed into margarine and other products. Your next-door neighbors are going to eat you for breakfast. The mind boggles that this is actually happening. It must be very difficult fully to realize the enormity of such a situation when it's occurring. It's difficult enough to believe it now. We know there were people whose minds didn't boggle. Some got out; some hid; some emigrated "internally." Some fought and were tortured horribly and killed. We have a word for someone who feels he is being persecuted when the majority view is that he is not being persecuted: *paranoia.* It's not oversimplifying to say that paranoia has to do with a feeling that you can't trust people, that, "in fact"—let's put *in fact* in quotation marks—it seems that you can trust no one, nothing. But there is no word for a situation where one can't bring oneself to realize that one *is being persecuted when one is.* Nor is there a word for persecuting people without realizing one is.

In the paranoid position, one thinks one is being persecuted when one is not; in the other position, one thinks he is being *not persecuted* when he is. The second position is where a lot of the Jews were; the first where a lot of ordinary Germans were. The Jews found it very difficult to believe that they were being persecuted by people they were not persecuting, who were thinking that they were being persecuted by the Jews, and in turn not persecuting them. They were convinced that the Jews were poisoning the Aryan race. *We* would say now that the Nazis were collectively paranoid, an institutionalized group paranoia. They delineated and proceeded to destroy a set of perfectly ordinary, peaceful people, "because" they thought these people were destroying them. Let's call the Nazis Set A and the Jews, Set B. Set A thought that Set B was destroying them when they weren't, and Set B didn't realize that they were being destroyed by Set A when they were. Incidentally, if you want to study "bystander apathy," go to Calcutta.

EVANS: You raised a very interesting problem of paranoia—believing something exists when it doesn't—and the lack of a word for the situation where you don't believe something exists when it does. An extraordinary example of this type of process may exist in the Watergate situation involving the administration of former President Nixon. In tracing Mr. Nixon's history, it seems that he believed, from the start, that the press and media representatives were hostile toward him. When he lost a governor's race in California, he made the statement, "Now you don't have Richard Nixon to kick around anymore." The widely publicized Watergate hearings on American television and the subsequent events received heavy press and media coverage. Even before the series of events that led to his resignation, he appeared to be an unpopular figure and was represented very badly in the press. He has even been accused of functioning within a paranoid system. Starting from that premise, from the kind of thing you were talking about a moment ago, was his reaction paranoid if, in fact, the press was out to get him, as he thought it was? Was this irrational on his part or a rational act? What would be your reaction to this?

LAING: A paranoid system? Clearly a very serious complicated system, a very interesting system that deserves the most serious scientific study, a system of communication, second to none, of utmost significance for the ecosystem of this planet. Similar complex systems exist in Russia and China. The Arab world is developing its version. I think that psychiatric terminology can best be laid aside in considering the properties of such systems, which include their input and output to other systems, and their own central processing. Psychiatric terminology is still a very crude way to classify people. So I'm not happy about talking without inverted commas of "paranoid" systems, and so forth.

EVANS: All right, we won't use the phrase at all.

LAING: Let's just try to describe one bit of it, or at least begin to try to move towards a description of this system. I'll be very interested in your impressions on this. Nixon and Kissinger (Brodine, 1972) have both written books in which they've said something about how they see things, about what they've done and what they're doing. I haven't read any of these books, but I've read extracts. I've ordered them recently, and discovered that they were in stock in only one small bookshop in London. Not because they were sold out, but because there was no demand for them. Kissinger, like many diplomats before him, wrote, before he was adopted by Nixon, that certain negotiations should be conducted by the accredited representatives of states, but that general "security" being what it is, these negotiations would be dummy ones: real deals would be conducted by behind-the-scenes negotiators, and to insure full "security," even the accredited state representatives might be better off not knowing they were negotiating dummy agreements.[1] Such tactics must mean that subsystems of the system are deceiving each other. This must lead to the loss of a great deal of information. We are liars. Believe us. The president, the vice-president, the secretary of state, the chief of staff, all represent vast complexes of deception and self-

[1] Stalin is credited with the remark that to regard diplomacy as compared to honesty rather than to deception would be comparable to regarding air as made of wood.

deception, apparently. One of the most extraordinary things about Watergate was the attempt to move in cumbersome apparatus, when a small device was all that was needed. Maybe Watergate was a set-up setup. All this corruption started long before Nixon. There's no fundamental surprise in this order after Shakespeare. You don't know who your enemy is, and there's no one you can call your friend. You try to find out everything about everyone. It is manifestly impossible. Who can spy on the spies of the spies? . . . Nixon should have been taken seriously when he said he was very upset to discover that the "secret" American policy involved in the SALT negotiations was known to the Russians in advance. He must have realized, knowing how "secret" that information was (or maybe it was leaked), that there was indeed a serious leak in his security system. There must be an army of people whose job it is to insure that the president of the United States can have conversations with people that no one else can hear. Why were the tapes not burned right away? Lenin carried Machiavelli's *The Prince* around in his pocket and went to sleep with it under his pillow—I think he died with it under his pillow. His closest associates were ferocious creatures like Trotsky. There's no question about the ferocity of the game. Never even dream of telling the truth. That is just a base line we take for granted. Keep the truth to yourself, just in case. You never know. Tell the truth sometimes however, when it doesn't matter, but make it appear to. Truth has disappeared. There is information and misinformation—all grist for taking advantage, whatever it might be, whenever it might turn up. No telling. You do know they're trying to find out what you think (but you don't know who they are). I might not even have thought of what they're after. The military are very interested in telepathy, hypnosis, et cetera. For over twenty years, this research has been sponsored by military establishments. God knows what the Chinese are up to in that respect. This is one of the potentially most important military weapons there is. Can EEG's influence at a distance? They do. There are indications that the EEG's of mothers show changes when their babies, miles away, are in sudden distress. There's a throb, or beat, a pulse between us that the grabby, manipulating fingers of the military-medical-scientific-industrial complex is just beginning to get hold of. The swamis are being wired up. Magic and voodoo? Primitive. Hitler had his astrologists. In fact, we now know that World War II was largely programmed, astrologically, by Hitler's astrological advisors. Churchill employed a state astrologer to advise him on what Hitler's astrologers were doing. These matters, institutionalized in the real scientific-political-industrial-military nightmare, are well beyond naïve gropings around. How could a president of the United States (after George Washington!) tell a lie?

Maybe someone is materializing someone in front of you, a five-channel synchronized hallucination! There are people around who claim they can do this. These are simplistic devices that can take up a bit of sound, for what use no one can possibly know. Cut out a *not*, or put in a *not*, you've changed the sense of a tape, such that no one can detect it. A system of communication based on lies, deceit, deception, decoying, attempts not to communicate, at any time, the truth of one's intentions, or what one is thinking, what one's next move is, what one thinks the others are getting people to suppose, that one is on a false track, pretending to believe, pretending not to, when one does, when one doesn't—it's too simple to believe that they're lying when they're putting forward as a lie what is really the truth. Hollywood scriptwriters did not invent such situations. This must be Nixon's world; it can't be otherwise. Anyone who wants to criticize Nixon should imagine—without being a utopian idealist—that he is in that position, with that form of power or importance, where it is possible that the chiefs of staff are pursuing a policy even a president or secretary cannot stop, let alone Congress or the Senate. It's quite possible that in certain "sensitive" areas certain people might feel that the policy they are pursuing is in the best interests of the United States, and the rest of the free world, and may be jeopardized if certain information were supplied to the president.

EVANS: There are those who look at Nixon and argue that he is particularly a victim of this kind of perceived vendetta against him. Presumably there's a sort of plausibility, in terms of the system you just described. In a sense, he sees himself as a victim of the media, and so he goes through all these steps that have since come to the surface in open hearings before millions of people. We had a previous example of this in the United States in the televised hearings involving the late Senator Joseph McCarthy. The destructive aspects of his style were brought out, and his denouement seemed to be a breath of fresh air. Not only in the United States, but perhaps never before in the history of the world, had millions of people been simultaneously exposed to such an understanding of something like this system you've described. However, it seems to me that the process you're describing is progressive, that you're implying that soon we will no longer be able to have any open human relationships.

LAING: I think that what we're having reported is the tip of an iceberg of a vast system of our communi-

cation. In my last book, *The Politics of the Family*
(Laing, 1971), there is a description of the rule systems of communication, some aspects of a set of rules
that would have to underpin a multitiered system of
lies. Some of it seemed to fit descriptions in the "Watergate thing" precisely. Yet my attempts to characterize such a rule system arose out of studies of families
in the U.K. In some families you could say that, more
or less, there's no a priori basis, that "truth" and "communication" have anything to do with each other. One
must disencumber one's mind of the naïve notion that,
for many people, communication necessarily has anything to do with being truthful. Truth can be *used* to
control. It can be used as a means to fight, by lies or
other devices. But suppose one is being controlled to
death, and the only way we can stop being controlled
and killed by others is to control them and kill them. If
someone's really going to enslave us, or kill us, or do
what he likes with us unless we stop him, we've got to
stop him. A large sector of history, not only recent versions, shows that as long as there have been people,
they have been killing others. The only thing that
seems to have stopped them was to be killed. The
Mongols did it until they were stopped. The holy wars
of Christianity did it. World War I was primarily just
who could kill the most, until it was agreed that both
sides had reached the limits of acceptability. The
white North Americans have virtually killed off all the
local inhabitants of North America. That's why they
are there. There's no one living on earth today who
isn't there on the basis of the people that have been
killed and destroyed by *our* forebears.

Now we know that. We know what we're like. We
know that's what we still do when we come up against
a culture that can't defend itself from us. They're

wiped out, utterly destroyed. Our "civilization" has pretty well destroyed every culture it's come across. It is only recently that anthropologists have managed to get this message through, even to a lot of other anthropologists. These other people are people no less intelligent than we are, maybe even more intelligent than we are, who have a different idea of living in the world than we have. It's not because they're genetically inferior, or on the brink of passivity, that they haven't surrounded themselves with the artifacts we have. At this moment some people are still out there, with few clothes or without clothes, in the environment of the sky, the sun, the wind, and the stars. We're not. We're sitting on top of wood, on top of asphalt, on top of a cellar surrounded by bricks, with the windows plugged up, with all sorts of plumbing, with electric lights and recording devices, when there's a garden with trees outside. The sun is shining and we're not in it. We're in an office, on the cut-up wood of dead trees that we're sitting on, that we have as our table. That's what we do with the world, entirely at our pleasure. We shall cut down God knows how many trees so we can have one edition of this book. The mind boggles at what we're doing. Things we have done will be done to us, for spite, for fun, with indifference, by people like us, unless we are more ferocious and smarter. The truth is only a pawn in the game of defending ourselves in every way possible. In this game, as Machiavelli, Metternich, and everyone who plays it knows, one of the most important tactics is deception. Deceive the enemy, put him on a false scent, and take every advantage you can when he's weakest.

EVANS: So, when you see something like Watergate, you see it as simply symptomatic of the whole process of destroying the other before he gets you, and this is just the most recent electronic reflection of the process?

LAING: Every decent American knows that the cavalry and traders, the people interfaced with American Indians, were pursuing our sometimes policy of ruthless genocide. They handed out blankets laced with typhus, in order to kill off the women and children by epidemics of infectious disease. So I've come to suppose, anyway. It wasn't reported in the newspapers of the time, as far as I know, but the people who got that together and the people who gave it out took precautions that there wouldn't be an inspection. Many people would be scandalized if they knew of the ongoing state of the game in many parts of the world. The worst barbarities are still perpetuated by "ourselves," by our "allies" and "friends." I'm not proposing or supporting what are commonly called revolutionary tactics, but how to diminish the degree of reciprocal threat, danger, fear, and so on. I would not put my gun down if I knew someone would shoot me if I did. If I thought he was going to pounce on me with a knife, I would reach for my gun, if I weren't as good a knifesman as he was, and shoot him before he got to me. If that's what it looked as if he were going to do, then he would be asking for it. That's our attitude, but I would like to be as disarmed as prudence allows. And that attitude offers them no more consolation than theirs does to us.

THE WORLD OPENS UP IN DIFFERENT WAYS

PART VI

Overview | In this section Dr. Laing and I discuss his recent visit to the Far East and his attempts to understand the ways in which people from widely differing cultures approach the experiences of the human mind. He describes some of his experiences, and the correlations and differences between Eastern and Western experience. Dr. Laing reacts to the idea of chemically induced states of consciousness, and we conclude this section with a discussion of his own involvement with meditative processes.

EVANS: Moving along to a slightly different area, Dr. Laing, I was most intrigued in my reading of your work, and in following your recent life, by a point you made about other types of cultures in which, perhaps, people are living a little closer to nature, in a more simple sense, with philosophies that are somewhat different from ours. Several months ago you were apparently looking at this whole question of human experience, and in searching more deeply into human experience, you went off to some of the Eastern countries to get a better feel of their views of reaching certain states of consciousness. As I understand it, you went to India and Ceylon—

LAING: Yes, India and Ceylon.

EVANS: Some of these practices that come from India— yoga, for example—involve meditative qualities that somehow seem to lull us away from the material world and bring us closer, perhaps, to ourselves and to our own conscious state. I am curious about the impact of such practices on the people of India, themselves. On the plane com-

ing into London I happened to be sitting next to a
very intelligent Indian engineer and we were talking
about such practices. I described you as someone who
had gone to India to learn more about this aspect of
the culture, and he said he'd like to know more about
it himself. Although he is living in India, he is just
about as far removed from this type of meditation, and
just as involved in engineering, as any American engineer would be. What, exactly, did you learn from your
experience there? Have any of your views changed?
Do you have a better understanding of where this sort
of thing is going, and perhaps why it is suddenly becoming so interesting to a greater proportion of contemporary Western society, even though it has by no
means saturated contemporary Indian culture?

LAING: As the world opens up in many different
ways, all sorts of spiritual and mental disciplines become visible to everyone, and are nothing like as remote as they once were. We in the West have a type
of practice (little practiced, little understood) called
psychoanalysis. We'd be very lucky if we could say
that the level of our culture is qualitatively better compared to some of these cultures in their heyday. Within
the context of other cultures, different ways developed
in which people investigated themselves, together
with different ways and methods of actually *experiencing* the human mind. This is a subject I'm interested in myself. I'm concerned with the loss of the
psyche, of the disintegration of structure of the psyche,
without saying we even know what it is. I have been
interested in involving myself close up with people who
had been in different experiences from my own. I met
a number of people in India and Ceylon I wouldn't
have met without going there, some people from the
old India, if you like. Of course, in contemporary
India, there are all kinds.

EVANS: This engineer we met on the plane, then, is really in a subculture different from those you were seeking to understand?

LAING: Yes. There's the industrial, technical, technological India, which belongs to a system that is the same the world over. And Indians function, very often, on several levels in different subcultures. I was with one Calcutta Indian family—he manufactures air-conditioning equipment—whose daughters speak no Indian language or dialect, only English. In another family the mother spoke no English, and the children no Indian; the father translated. They might have one or two records of Ravi Shankar, as I do, but it's the Beatles and whatnot you hear. But you can walk on the street and there are cows, people chanting—people dying on the pavement. There are extremes of everything in India, all at once, and that is one of the extraordinary experiences of India. Some Indians believe they have achieved a sort of synchronism of hierarchical differentials so that they can look at all these things, interpenetrating and coexisting over a thousand years of differences between people who are living and dying in the extremes of poverty and extremes of wealth, who live out extremes of lying and the pursuit of knowledge, or indifference to it all. I met, and stayed with for a few weeks, a man who lived up in the Himalayan foothills under a jutting rock, a sort of crag. He had a fire going, he kept that going, thank God, in the middle of winter—very cold, sleet and snow —his only clothes a loincloth. He never ate except what was brought to him. He made a point of eating roughly once a day while I was there, an indulgence he regarded as a rather excessive concession to a guest. This man was a medical doctor. He was now in his fifties. At twenty-nine he had gone off to the wilderness. He had been brought up by a French lady, a niece of Na-

poleon. He spoke French and English very well, San-
skrit, different Indian dialects, a bit of Japanese, a bit
of German. He was an orthodox Hindu. It's difficult, of
course, to say what an orthodox Hindu is, because
there are so many sorts of orthodoxies within Hindu-
ism, but he was very much, within one of the primary
systems of Hindu orthodoxy, recognized as a swami.
He went off into the wilderness of jungles and mountains and lived there for over seven years without seeing a human being and then came back and stationed
himself about an hour's walk from the nearest village,
unapproachable by car. He was there where anyone
who wanted to could come see him. He sat and sang.

EVANS: Were your wife and children with you?

LAING: They joined us for a weekend, but most of
the time they were in a family house some distance
away.

EVANS: So you took off on this—it sounds almost
like a pilgrimage—this meeting with a many-faceted
person who somehow has tried to experience, in a very
simple sense, an entire culture that he himself, even as
an Indian, had never experienced before. Are you saying that he was going through all these years as a kind
of reconsideration of his own identity?

LAING: He's fifty-one now, and he grew up in a
combination of grass-roots Indian culture and Western
culture of the most sophisticated kind. He grew up
playing the piano and the organ, he even learned the
bagpipes. And he was brought up as a Roman Catho-
lic. His mother and father were Indians, and his father
was a colonel of a regiment. He was interesting to me
because he had actually experienced in his own life,
synchronously from childhood, both the original Indian experience—he hadn't been cut off from that—and
the Western thing. As I mentioned, he graduated as a

doctor and practiced medicine, and knew Indian medicine as well. He was very fond of fast cars and had enjoyed driving a Mercedes along Indian roads—an amazing thing. Then one day he left all that activity in which he felt he was just driving around. . . .

EVANS: These things began to seem pointless to him, then?

LAING: He felt if he didn't get away from human beings for a while he would go completely crazy. Even after recuperating from them for seven years, he still felt that one had to be pretty well grounded to be able to take the normal insane human species for long.

EVANS: What you're really saying is that he was suddenly touched by a deeper conception of life than prevailed in India. What did you learn from this?

LAING: There's no sort of formula that encapsulates it. I enjoyed very much the companionableness of another man who had stationed himself in the world in a position that touched mine in many ways, and yet was vastly different. I think he confirmed me in the politics of experience without knowing anything of the explicitness of the thing I was coming from. It was the same sort of experience that I had with Gregory Bateson. He had the most distinctive perceptual capacities of anyone that I've met, and to see someone like him observing other human beings, to be with someone who is taking in more than usual and putting out more than usual, to get the feel of just what they're picking up and seeing, and the edge that they have on even the quickest of their contemporaries, but had also become *calm,* was a great consolation.

EVANS: In addition to this experience with such a unique person—and it's fascinating the way you've been speaking of it as almost an analogue of yourself and Bateson—what other experiences struck you?

You've mentioned that you were seeking a better understanding of the meditative processes that are analogous to psychoanalysis in our culture. Were you able
to get into this? It's probably quite a bit different from
some of the Western versions, with teen-agers en-
rolling in yoga classes and going to yoga retreats, as
many of them do. In fact, my own daughter was on
one this past summer, and it was an interesting thing
to her. She reported that they had many silent days
when there was actually no talking, and that they
would get up in the morning and go through certain
rituals. It's the sort of experience that has attracted a
wide and diverse group of American college and high
school students. Now if you go to India and try to seek
out this same thing, as you did, obviously the impression that you gain is far different from that of an
American teen-ager who participates for a matter of a
few weeks.

LAING: I wouldn't say that I went to India in order
to find their meditational practices. I reckon that I
discovered, as a child, without being taught by anyone
at all, that there are different ways of resting and
flexing and employing one's mind. I used to spend a lot
of time just sitting, looking into the fireplace. You
could call that fire *kasina*, if you heard someone calling
it by the Buddhist name; one could speak about or
codify different stages of absorption that the mind goes
through and the phenomenology of that. As one continues to look at the fire, or candle, or any object, without turning away from it, but looking at it steadily for
a certain period of time, this particular form of meditation, focused attention, meditation on one subject,
yields well-documented mental transforms. You can,
stare at a wall, you can meditate upon a paradox that
is impossible to solve, you can think the unthinkable.

People have different procedures which have been developed in different parts of the world. Now they are in general circulation. The device, for instance, of not talking for a while—there's a lot of this to be found around the corner anywhere. Mantras are normal parts of the usual lives of millions of Indians, still. In India, now, these things are parts of one of many coexisting cultures. When the Indian westernizes, he or she picks up his or her Indiana from the bookshops, the way any Westerner does. The same kind of guru systems develop for Indians. The big-name gurus in India are not all that different to many Indians than they are to Americans. You have Indian celebrities, like American celebrities, who are in the same sort of role relationship to comparable subcultures.

EVANS: Of course, some of them have come to the United States.

LAING: A village boy, who looks good and knows how to keep his mouth shut and just continues to stand, walk, sit, not eat too much, and sleep, sit, stand, walk—not doing anything. Don't lift a finger to do anything. If you can get away with it, and look sufficiently beautiful, you are, in India, in a position, if you are noticed, where people turn and wonder if this guy is a holy man or a phony. And that man you met on the plane may look like a Westerner, but he is also an Indian. In Indian newspapers there will be pages of advertisements on marriages, on sales of daughters to this family or that family: high-caste (naming the caste) male engineer, B.S., two thousand rupees a month going to four thousand rupees by age forty-five, with pension, seeks high-caste Indian girl, graduate if possible; and it may state certain accomplishments, play a musical instrument, or this thing, or that thing; astrological charts required. Such advertisements are also modern India. It has a slightly different inflection in style of doing from New York and London.

EVANS: You were equating these meditative processes with psychoanalysis—that this is our own meditative process arising in our culture—and of course, there are many others as well. But actually, you have several dimensions here that stand side by side. There is the type of meditative process that you describe, which is really reacting to a certain kind of stimulus—gazing, attempting to move away from the immediate sensory response, and perhaps, as you gaze at a candle, allowing some sort of increasing impact of a purer conscious state, whatever that means. You could, of course, induce this with drugs to some degree. . . .

LAING: I doubt if it's the same thing.

EVANS: Yes, but that's the question I was getting at. To what degree, in fact, can this sort of thing be reproduced with drugs? Now LSD and other drugs, such as mescaline, have been used both in research and for "trips" among young people. In what respects can you duplicate this kind of stimulus-induced state? I'm talking about reproducing environmental-stimulus induced states as against actual chemically induced states.

LAING: I think it's too simplistic to define or characterize this state as a stimulus-induced state.

EVANS: All right. Expand on that a little.

LAING: If we do that, we have to talk about the auto-stimulus of the brain, or stimulus of itself, when feedback is part of the stimulus-induced state, because there are many different sorts of meditational practices. The one I was talking about (it's often thought appropriate for "beginners") is the one which, with practice, all one's total, complete, undivided attention is brought to bear completely on one subject.

EVANS: You're talking about an environmental object, now?

LAING: It could be a mental object. It could be located in one's mind. It could be a triangle, a dot, a circle. . . .

EVANS: Sort of internal-external. All right, fine. Now that defines it more clearly. How would that type of state then differ from a chemically induced state, as you see it?

LAING: There's no such thing as a chemically induced state of total fixed absorption, as far as I know. One can't take a chemical and achieve instant mental discipline. It might facilitate some things, but everything's chemical. The state we're in right now is chemical. If one put in another chemical, it's another chemical state, so it's one chemical state or another chemical state.

EVANS: Well, that's a good way of putting it.

LAING: And you might say that one chemical state is artificial and the other is like, for example, the relationship to our stomach and gastrointestinal-alimentary system before we add food. If we don't take any food for three days, we will be in another sort of state. If we don't take any food, except water, for seven days, we're in another state. And if we take some mescaline now, before a meal, after a meal, after sleep, before sleep, that's another state. If we don't sleep for seven days, for more than an hour a day, as I was doing—

EVANS: You were not sleeping for more than an hour—

LAING: For more than an hour a day, and not because I was making a conscious effort. It was just sort of a lightness. I was hardly sleeping at all for months. I had begun by bringing my attention to bear

in a sustained way. First of all, it takes a lot of practice
to do it for one second. Going back to it, after I
stopped doing it naïvely in childhood, I tried off and
on for some years before I got it again—just fully undivided attention, without even any millisecond flashes
of anything else. Any sort of thing your mind focuses
on for just a split second, at that decisive moment, your
mind is absolutely synchronized with the object of
consciousness, whether it's a sight, or a taste or a smell,
external stimuli or internal stimuli, of any kind you
suppose. I would say that it's the same in any state of
consciousness, because there's no bright light, no fi-
nality, after one second, two seconds, three seconds,
one minute, two minutes. There are very few people in
the world, I would say, who have got minds that they
can just move into a sustained twenty-minutes, on-cue
fixed attention on any object, and out again, with complete effortlessness. The mind is often compared to an
elephant that's in heat, tied with a rope to a stake, con-
tinually struggling to get away from it, tugging at it.
The mind goes away from you, you bring it back, it
goes away again. When you finally get it settled down,
to rest itself, as it were, upon an object, then there are
nonverbal transformations of mind that occur then,
absolutely straightforward and continuing. They've
been mapped out in extraordinary scholastic detail by
people who've spent their time just fixing their mind
on one object. If you can do that for twenty-four
hours at a stretch, if you keep on doing it, essentially
it continues. Surprising! It doesn't necessarily make
one a better person, and it still is only "practice." But
the point is, to me, going into the state induced by
such practice is a procedure that is a different sort of
attitude from psychoanalysis. In this particular procedure it's not a question of theory, or what you think

about, or what your motivation or intentions are, or what you think you're going to put into it or get out of it. All that's entirely irrelevant. You just do it. You're given a recipe, and you follow that recipe precisely, and such and such things will happen at different stages of the "baking" procedure. You can pick up different corollaries of this in an EEG of monks who have been meditating for five hours a day for years. Certain theta rhythms have become apparent in people that have been at it for six weeks, or six days, but it takes longer to get into the deeper stages, in which, apparently, the whole central nervous system starts to find some different throb. Something changes. This state of mind, this very restful state of mind, with no discursive thoughts arising, no body images present, no conscious processing of sense-data, no distinctions being made since no binary operating is going on at a level that is being consciously recorded, is a very restful state, indeed. But I don't think it proves anything, metaphysically, ontologically, or existentially.

A CAPACITY FOR UNCERTAINTY, MYSTERY, AND DOUBT

PART VII

Overview | In this section Dr. Laing describes the concept and implementation of experimental therapeutic communities, such as Kingsley Hall in London, offering some insights gained from this experiment, and commenting on the alternatives to the traditional mental hospital. We discuss his role in contemporary psychiatry, as he perceives it, and he reacts to his critics, particularly in the areas of drug usage and the psychedelic model of psychosis. In conclusion Dr. Laing takes an interesting, and enigmatic, look at the future.

EVANS: Dr. Laing, I think that a number of people in the fields of psychiatry, psychology, and social work have become acutely aware of the circularity of the mental hospital, essentially training so-called mentally ill people to become good mental hospital patients. This criticism is directed not only to the earlier years, when treatment was often abusive and vicious, but there are those who say that the patronizing, almost too gentle, concern about patients that characterizes some hospitals today is probably equally bad. Both systems seem to be doing the same thing, that is simply training people to adjust to this environment, which has nothing to do with rehabilitating these individuals in the sense of resocializing them. I know that one of the answers that you had to this type of criticism was a venture in, for want of a better term, what we could call the therapeutic community at Kingsley Hall.[1] I understand that in 1970 Kingsley Hall was finally closed

[1] For a brief description of the Philadelphia Association, which coordinates these therapeutic communities, see Appendix B.

in the sense that you had come to the end of an experimental period.

LAING: All that was there still goes on. There are actually seven households like Kingsley Hall in London right now. It's an exfoliation of Kingsley Hall. Kingsley Hall was simply the name of the building. We leased it for five years in 1965.

EVANS: I'm glad to have you clear this up, because in a recent film this had been perceived as being the end of an experimental period.

LAING: Oh, the *Asylum* film that you were showing at your—

EVANS: American Psychological Association meeting—

LAING: Yes, that's a film that was made in 1971.

EVANS: Very briefly, because I know it would be impossible to do justice to this, what are the general patterns of these "Kingsley Halls" that seem to be an effective means of dealing with some individuals, in contrast to what goes on in a traditional mental hospital?

LAING: I don't want to say *in contrast* to what goes on in a traditional mental hospital. I've never put down traditional mental hospitals in the blanket condemnation sort of way that some people have. There are people in all these institutions that we are talking about, and, in a certain sense, nothing else except people moving and talking in relationship to each other in different sorts of reciprocally defined roles in social space. People are interplaying with people in and out of mental hospitals. Many people who stay in our households are usually people who might well be in mental hospitals—very often, I would say—and they're not staying because there's anything special or even particularly pleasant about the households, but for these people almost anywhere is better than a mental hospital, from their own experience. Goffman, in a conversation I had with him a few years ago—we were talking about the future of theory and observation in this field—said that he thought that really the thing that would add something I couldn't get otherwise to both my experience and theory of what this was about would be to put myself in a mental hospital, as a patient, anonymously, and just get the feel of it. To him it was literally a scene of sheer horror. I would consider, if I was well paid for it, spending a day or two as a prisoner to see what it was like. I would have to have absolute guarantees that once in, I could really get out, and be absolutely convinced that it wasn't a setup, and that I could stick it out for, say, three days, if I knew I would get out then, and be well rewarded for it. But I wouldn't take three days of my chances in any mental hospital I know of by choice. That's speaking personally. It doesn't matter who happens to be on duty. A nurse, or whoever is on duty, has the power to order an assault on my chemical system, at the very least, routinely, perhaps. I would regard it as pretty horrible if it was happening when I wanted to keep my mind clear and felt I needed all my wits about me, and they were systematically being taken away from me because it was thought not good for me to have access to my own mind, feelings, and senses.

EVANS: These households have been described as communelike in structure. Would this be a fair statement?

LAING: Yes. All the things that have been happening since we started this specifically, in 1964–1965, are experimental and remain experimental. If I state the principle of it, it can be put very simply. My impression, out of my years of psychiatric practice and experience, is that the main single thing that really makes a difference to people who are in a state of distress is to come across another human being who is really there, as a real presence to him. That is very rare. I recall watching a film of Jane Fonda speaking before some congressional hearing because of her views on Vietnam, and the Hanoi appearance. She was talking about the bombs falling, and the women and children and the plastic shrapnel. You know, you can't pick the plastic shrapnel out with X ray or anything, and it's particularly designed to give people a slow, painful life—it doesn't quite kill you, but if it hits you, you're in agony the rest of your life. It's used to demoralize the civilian population. And she was describing this, and the camera was panning the audience, the faces of the court, the people in the corridor, the policeman standing in the hall, and you could see it was grabbing just one or two of them, just by a slight look of attentiveness you could see it was actually affecting them—not complete Zonksville, you know—but just giving a bit of an ear to it. It was all just like that. That's the medium in which someone's trying to say something that she believed in, and that was true, but if no one listens to you—no one, which quite easily happens—you're a minority of one. You're like the ancient mariner trying to tell his story to the wedding guest, who doesn't really want to hear. If you detain him, then off you go to get tranquilized, and you're in a very tight spot, indeed, a very desperate spot until all that stuff is taken away and someone says, all right, I'm leveling with you. In this space with me you've got sanctuary or asylum. I'm not going to do anything *to* you. You can come into my space if you're not too frightened, and you can walk out again if you want to. I'm not going to stop you. I might kick you out of my space if I don't want you, but you're free to come and go with me up to the distance I'm prepared to go, and here I am. One hopes there are a sprinkling of people around in every mental hospital—maybe the cleaning woman or the cook, or the superintendent—who are still just human beings.

Suddenly, there's someone there who you can see is *safe* to be with, who has no harmful intentions toward you, doesn't want to do anything to you, doesn't want to *treat* you, doesn't feel that you've got to be kept there for your own good. I'm not talking of prison. That's another story. But it is very confusing if a place of hospitality (a hospital) is a prison—even a special prison—but a prison, not a haven, an asylum, a refuge, a check-out place, a sanctuary. You come there and the doors are locked. You're not allowed to go out. All right, you know that. It's quite simple. In our experimental places we've tried to do without "roles." I'm not sure that doing without the roles really improves matters or is possible. That's not the essential of the thing. It's experimenting with social form so that we can find within the context of our social system the best sanctuary, wherein a nexus of relationships can subsist. One is frightened; in order not to be frightened, to become unfrightened, one has got to feel safe at the same depth in one's bone marrow as one was afraid. When you're freaked out by something, when the mind has gone off into a boggle, a spin, it's got locked, jammed, disconnected, you've got to be able to feel safe at the same depth as the terror. It's got to be OK, it's got to be safe. And the most important thing in an environment, as far as safety goes, is the people in it. So we try to experiment with how *we* can, in our context, be safe people for other people to meet. When we don't know people, people we've never met before, we have to show by our presence that we are not going to do anything to anybody in the name of anything.

EVANS: Dr. Laing, we've pursued some of the things that as a social psychologist, I think are among your most significant contributions, but what do *you* believe to be your most significant ones?

LAING: I hope that I haven't yet made what might be my most significant contributions. I see myself in the skeptical tradition of Western thought. That's to say, to look at the nature of matter, the nature of man, the nature of the mind, the nature of phenomena directly, without presuppositions, to suspend judgment, as practiced in the Greek schools. Husserl (1952) picks this up directly in his phenomenology, and I think exactly the same as Freud practiced in his "free association" (German: *Einfall*, literally incoming, coming in, occurrence, whatever occurs to me). That's a discipline in the spirit of Keats's negative capacity— what he calls the capacity for uncertainty, mystery, and doubt, rather than certainty, objectification, and having arrived at the answers. In other words, I think it's a tremendously important thing I wrestle with in my mind, not to supply my lack of knowledge—the gaps in what I really know from my immediate, direct sight, sound, taste, touch, smell, but the information I get is all I have to go on, all that anyone's got to go on —not to fill the gaps, by beliefs one then has to defend since they are imperiled. That's the beginning of fanaticism, and I attribute a great deal of the world's woes to that propensity I recognize in my own mind, and that of other people, to become convinced that one is right, that the questions are finally answered, one has seen the final revelation, one has seen the Vision, the Angel, seen God, been redeemed, the water is moved, and one has crossed over to the other shore— that one has achieved enlightenment. I'm not preaching cynicism, or nihilism, or what the fuck, either. I wish I could say it. *"Auriga sepa los caminos y nunca llega a Cordoba"* (Lorca).[2]

EVANS: But you've applied this skepticism to certain specific things that you considered important. Now am I correct in saying that you've applied this skepticism to the classification of mental disorders and, more specifically, to schizophrenia, to the problem of how really to understand the family, to the problem of—

LAING: —everything—

EVANS: —the hospital. Everything that you've done—

LAING: Everything. Not just everything that I've dealt with—everything. All phenomena without exception, mental phenomena like the phenomena of mathematics, imagination, music, art; the phenomena of memory, of dreams, of waking perception, of sensation; the phenomena of thought, ideas, and anything else you'd like to mention, the phenomena of the external world where science goes on. In other words, without exception, the whole data the human mind has before it. Remember Plato's conclusion:

"Let this much be said: and further let us affirm what seems to be the truth, that, whether one is or is not, one and the others in relation to themselves and one another, all of them, in every way, are and are not, and appear to be and appear not to be."

EVANS: Well . . .

LAING: . . . this cannot be another orthodoxy . . .

EVANS: . . . as you know . . .

LAING: . . . but I mean to look at things, at the meal, not the menu, at the territory, not the map.

EVANS: I see.

2 "The coachman may know the roads and never arrive at Cordoba."

LAING: You could apply the same thing to the phenomena of astronomy.

EVANS: As you know, you have been subjected to a great deal of criticism both by colleagues in psychiatry and by people in various other fields, and you certainly must be aware of these criticisms. It would be only fair to hear, first, which of these criticisms has troubled you the most, and second, what your reaction to some of these specific criticisms might be.

LAING: There are two areas to which I'm particularly sensitive because there are two areas of my own uncertainty and indecision, and there are also areas in which I feel unhappy that I've been attacked. I think some of it is based on misunderstandings on the part of my critics, and a failure to read a bit more accurately what I actually wrote. Some people have felt that I thought it enhanced one's wisdom to take drugs like acid, mescaline, and whatnot, that it was a recommended part of the curriculum of somebody who wished to understand the full human story, that really you couldn't expect to enter into reality, or have much to say, unless you'd taken a trip. There's a great deal of confusion about the psychedelic model of psychosis, and stuff like that. I couldn't begin—well, I could begin just now, but there isn't time to get very far in disentangling what I think are some of the gross confusions around that area. I hope I can manage to get myself, in the next few months, to write something in which I at least try to state my own position about that, to disclaim many of the positions that have been attributed to me.

EVANS: You mention the psychedelic model of psychosis. Are you referring here to what some writers have called your psychedelic theory of schizophrenia? That becoming schizophrenic is a type of trip in the same sense that there is a drug trip, and upon returning from this trip, the person will be miraculously cured? Is this the sort of thing to which you're referring?

LAING: We'd have to take my answer to that within the context of the way we've dealt with the concept of schizophrenia before. You'd have to move that out of the way. There are some people, who for reasons best known to God knows whom, figure as my informants and friends, like this chap, Jesse Watkins, who's written his autobiography. A number of people who have gone into this type of experience and who have afterwards taken acid feel that there is a big overlap. There are many people diagnosed as schizophrenic who would disagree completely. It used to be a clinical adage in Scotland, where I was brought up in psychiatry, that maybe thirty percent of people diagnosed as schizophrenic remit, if left to themselves to go through whatever it is they are going through. Such people might lie huddled up, completely regressed— thump the wall in a padded cell where they would piss and shit where they lay. There were some cells in most hospitals where people could do that, and some people would come in every few years, some only once, and go through this sort of thing. After three months or so, they would be out again and functioning in society at large. Some people were seen as having recurrent numbers like this, and the "good" clinician could recognize them. The modern clinician can't recognize these people, because he's never allowed to see them. *He never sees the natural history of the condition or conditions* all this controversy is about because it is frozen by the "tranquilizers," ECT, or whatnot, even in research places. There must be very few (if any) places in the whole of the United States where people are "allowed" to go through numbers like this. If only as pure science, just to see the natural history.

EVANS: Our time is coming to a close rapidly. I am wondering what things you are working at now. What are you planning to do in the future? What hopes do you have for the sort of things that start with this very skeptical frame of reference you have just described? What will you be studying next that you think will be worthy of your attention and concern?

LAING: Well, what is more worthy of my attention and concern than the self, the human heart, intellect, emotions, and/or physicality? I was having a conversation with my son Adam, who is five years old, and we were playing a game,

ADAM: How would you like it . . . if I cut off both your arms and both your legs and your head?

ME: And if I did that to you, where would you be?

He put his hand on his heart, which is where the Greeks felt the psyche, the feeling, really resided, and he said, "Here, of course." He's not out of his head at all. He's just right there. Then he said to me, "Suppose I took your body and cut it up into little pieces. Where would you be then?" For all my psychological knowledge, I don't know. I said, "You tell me." He couldn't tell me either. Where is one's heart?

APPENDIXES

APPENDIX A

A CRITIQUE OF KALLMANN'S AND SLATER'S GENETIC THEORY OF SCHIZOPHRENIA
by R. D. Laing

> It may now be regarded as established that hereditary factors play a predominant role in the causation of schizophrenic psychoses.
>
> > W. Mayer-Gross, E. Slater, and M. Roth,
> > *Clinical Psychiatry*, 1954, p. 219

This view is probably still held by the majority of psychiatrists; and it is still standard teaching in many medical and nursing schools in all parts of the world.

Since no evidence for a "pathological process" has been directly forthcoming from pathology itself, support for the "organic pathology theory" has been sought in the genetic theory. The genetic theory, as we shall see, is in turn held to be supported by the organic pathology theory. These two theories do not, however, as is claimed, reciprocally validate each other. Rubbing together two phantom flints produces only the illusion of fire.

When it is claimed that the genetic theory of schizophrenia can be taken as "established," it is to the work of Franz Josef Kallman and Eliot Slater in particular that reference continues to be made.

Here we shall address ourselves particularly to the validity of the diagnostic procedures used by these two investigators. This will entail consideration of related aspects of their work, but our focus is on *diagnosis*.[1]

[1] Problems of sampling, establishing ovularity, the "correction" of raw figures, and the interpretation of the corrected figures have been critically considered in a number of papers, notably by Bleuler (1955), Planansky (1955), Alanen (1958), Jackson (1960), and Rosenthal (1959, 1961).

THE WORK OF KALLMANN

The writings of both Kallmann and Slater are often highly polemical. Kallmann, especially, interlaces his "objective findings" with interesting revelations of his state of mind. Although hypothesis, denunciation, theory, exhortation, and fact are so woven into the warp and woof of the work we have to review, I shall nevertheless try in this essay, as far as possible, to disentangle sheer polemics from "evidence."

Kallmann's one monograph exclusively devoted to schizophrenia was published in 1938. The first paragraph sets the tone that will be maintained throughout.

He begins with an urgent and impassioned appeal to genetic and to biological principles. "The battle," according to him, is going on on many fronts and

> . . . the key position of this battle seems to be held by the disease group of schizophrenia, which continues to crowd mental hospitals all over the world and affords an unceasing source of maladjusted cranks, asocial eccentrics and the lowest types of criminal offenders. (p. xiii)

Kallmann, as we shall see, has a colorful "descriptive" vocabulary for schizophrenia. He goes on:

> Even the faithful believers in the predominance of individualistic liberty, theoretically opposed to every eugenic measure in behalf of society as a whole, will admit that mankind would be much happier without those numerous adventurers, fanatics and pseudosaviors of the world who are found again and again to come from the schizophrenic genotype, and without that immoderate and pitiful misery which burdens the families tainted with schizophrenia. (p. xiii)

In Kallmann's "scientific" monograph table upon table of "objective statistics" are assembled to demonstrate the menace to society of these tainted degenerates. Exhortations for eugenic measures to halt their "unchecked propagation" and edifying homilies on the therapeutic, economic, ad-

ministrative, legal, biological implications of his "findings"
appear to be confused by the author with scientific presentation of data.

Although these have no *logical* bearing on the validity of
his work, they are an inextricable part of his presentation
both of his primary data and of his "findings" (i.e. after the
statistical "correction" of his data).

Above all, we must not forget the *expense*.

> We must remember that the prevention of several hun-
> dred schizophrenic patients and their tainted descend-
> ants, in every state, would save millions of dollars *for
> cultural purposes* [?!] and would considerably advance
> the biological qualities of future generations.

> Although it is the primary duty of medicine to care for
> the weak and the diseased, the obligation to protect the
> continuance of biologically sound families has become of
> major importance in our present era of declining birth
> rates. There can be no progress in culture, ethics and
> medicine so long as we neglect to improve the biological
> foundations of mankind and continue to accept genera-
> tions that are neither able nor willing to make rational
> use of their individual liberty and of all the gifts granted
> by high levels of science and art, religion and philosophy.
> (italics mine) (p. xiii)

This aspect of Kallmann is worth at least a thoughtful
pause, before we go on to consider the more apparently
"scientific" features of his work.

Kallmann drew his original material from a state mental
hospital in Berlin. The probands were admitted there in the
first decade of its existence (1893–1902), and the relatives,
ancestors, and descendants cover roughly a period from the
mid-nineteenth century to the early nineteen-thirties. From
our point of view it is not possible to understand the social
fact of schizophrenia (and this includes Kallmann himself
of course) without setting it in the socioeconomic context
of that hundred years in the history of Berlin. Kallmann
never so much as mentions such considerations, although
his book could well be read as a companion to *Wozzek*.

The greater number of these patients were "vagabonds," or "domestics": Kallman tells us that among all the individuals studied

> . . . we never find that we are dealing with top-notchers in their special field. In not a single case is there any outstanding excellence. *At best, we have the average man— one who would have been no loss to the world* if his schizophrenic parent had remained childless. [!] (italics mine) (p. 32)

Much of this book is occupied with eugenic considerations. Kallmann in this study and in his later writings warns against the naïve use of eugenic legislation in the attempt to eliminate schizophrenia. As he points out, the fertility rate of schizophrenics is below average anyway, and the higher than average familial incidence of schizophrenia extends to uncles, aunts, cousins, nephews, nieces, and apparently nonschizophrenic parents have schizophrenic children. Kallmann is, however, quite convinced that only persons with a specific gene defect can be schizophrenic, and that this defect is passed on by apparently "normal" carriers. The practical implications of this theory are revealed in many passages, of which the following are typical.

He is alarmed that what he regards as the "disease-onset" is on average 4.6 years prior to first commitment to mental hospital.

> This is a very important consideration from the standpoint of eugenics, for it must be one of our principal aims to cut down this interval in the future if eugenic prophylaxis in the heredity-circle of schizophrenia is to have measurable results. . . . Undoubtedly . . . whole series of marriages with schizophrenics would be quite simply prevented if in the future the disease were diagnosed at an early stage, and commitment made more promptly. (p. 27)

Kallmann regards the proper "treatment" for schizophrenia to be early internment, and *continual* internment for the rest of life, at least until past the reproductive period.

> It is generally known that even today the commitment of many schizophrenics occurs tardily. The blame for the delay lies in the prejudice of the lay public against psychiatric institutions, as well as in the failure of some officials and physicians to understand the nature of schizophrenic psychoses . . . the battle against these long-standing prejudices, which still oppose the prompt hospitalization of the insane, must be an important point in any effective program of eugenics. (pp. 27–28)

He must be a very worried man, now that tranquilizers, etc., have taken the place of padded cells, and patients are often free to have sexual intercourse.

The wretched fate of these patients, even in this century, can suitably be compared with the worst forms of inhumanity in the annals of human persecution. Herded into such a state mental hospital (albeit somewhat tardily), they died at an average age of 49.4 years, a high percentage from tuberculosis, a fact that Kallmann sees as "conclusive evidence" for a genetic deficit common to schizophrenia and tuberculosis. He still has not given up this hypothesis (see below).

The comparison of Kallmann's fanaticism, dressed up in his endless tables of figures, with the Inquisitor, is disturbingly fitting. Not only is it an "established fact" for him ". . . that the descendants of schizophrenics, both actual [!] and potential, should be regarded as eugenically undesirable, and therefore kept at the lowest possible number" (p. 47), but, as we shall see again and again, the whole circle of genotype-phenotype is so hermetically sealed, and so cut adrift from any reference to objective data, that any conceivable upset (or none) from dyspepsia to little more than running up the street (see the case of Hilda and Mary below) will be taken as evidence of the schizophrenia genotype. One should never forget that the status of this concept is utterly different in the realm of schizophrenia than in the case of Huntington's chorea or phenylpyruvic-acid dementia, etc. These are known organic illnesses, that is, the clinical hypothesis that they are "diseases" has been validated. That people who are diagnosed as schizophrenic are organically diseased is a completely unsubstantiated hypothesis. It cannot be converted into a "fact" in order to substantiate another completely unsubstantiated hypothesis (of genetic etiology), which is in turn converted into a "fact" in order to substantiate the organic hypothesis. With this "logic" behind him, Kallmann warns that

> . . . girls in the first stages of schizophrenia (diagnosed very often as "nervousness") are not warned against early marriage, but rather are advised to marry as the best remedy for a "nervous breakdown." (p. 48)

He is still pursuing the same theme in 1953.

> A young man, seeking the advice of a marriage counselor, may be so naïve as to appear more perturbed by what he calls his fiancée's "bad family history" (a few strokes, brain tumors, or institutionalized cases of senile dementia in grandparents and the husbands of favorite aunts) than he is by the fact that she had "a nervous breakdown which required only a few months of hospitalization while she was still in school." In line with this unknowing way of reasoning, the matrimonial prospects of a potential alcoholic or suspected drug addict tend to be less impaired than those of a bright young man who —apart from the deforming residues of a mastoid operation or a fairly mild poliomyelitic attack in childhood— comes from a family where the father died of general paresis in a mental hospital, and the mother committed suicide after having had several stillbirths and one congenitally blind child. (1953, p. 252)

He fortunately has still not managed to recognize

> . . . the homozygotic predisposition to schizophrenia before its clinical manifestation, and if possible, before the beginning of the reproductive period. At the mo-

ment, it is more than doubtful whether psychiatry will ever find a practical solution for this problem. We can only say with assurance that the scientist who may some day achieve the goal will earn the everlasting gratitude of all people for his contribution to the advancement of eugenics. (1938, p. 57)

The relatives of schizophrenics are often frightened that they will "pass it on" if they have children. We shall see in our studies how this can be understood.

Kallmann is against compulsory sterilization "on human, medical and methodological grounds," but rather

> We are . . . inclined to believe that in countries with high ethical standards and moral discipline, the liberty of the individual to determine his own fate within the limits of his natural sovereign rights, and the voluntary submission of every citizen to public measures adopted for the perpetuation of common happiness and security, belong to the finest and most indestructible ideals of mankind. Accordingly, the methods of education in biology, official bureaux of eugenic guidance and marriage counsel, mandatory health certificates before marriage and, if necessary, legal prohibition of marriage, seem preferable to us both on personal and scientific grounds. The objects of eugenics would then be well served, possibly better than by any other means, and sterilization might be held in reserve for the eugenically dangerous cases of "incorrigibles." In any case the problem of limiting the propagations of germinally affected transmitters of the predisposition to schizophrenia must first be solved in one way or another, if the eugenic campaign against this disease is ever to be successful. (p. 69)

It is just these fantasies that tend to be self-fulfilling prophecies, which Kallmann is only too eager to encourage.

> It is, indeed, quite probable that the offspring of our probands practiced deliberate birth-control to a large extent. This conclusion seems partly justified by the extraordinary drop in the birth rate from our proband generation to the next. Moreover, it agrees with the interest-

ing fact observed during our investigation that a number of the contemporary descendants of schizophrenics voluntarily refrain from having children in view of the hereditary taint in the family. It happened quite frequently that, in questioning descendants of our probands, we received the reply that they had remained single, or at any rate, had not wanted to have children, *because* they were afraid that these would be "idiots or insane." In one form or another, we heard such statements as, "I wanted to save my children from ending in an asylum like my mother," or "I'm not fit for marriage and dare not have children." Such opinions were repeated again and again, and they naturally suggested that certain eugenic concepts may already have automatically established their values in some tainted families. To be sure, their motives generally arose from purely personal or family consideration, and their practical effect can by no means become extensive enough to bring about an adequate check on the reproduction of schizophrenic families. (pp. 70–71)

With regard to the group of half-brothers and half-sisters of schizophrenics, the eugenic procedure should be the same as in the full-siblings of probands. In so far as they are phenotypically recognizable taint-carriers, they should be restrained from propagation. We must remember the finding of our fertility study, that the predisposition to schizophrenia is transmitted, to a large degree, through the collateral lines; in addition, we shall see in the next section that the disease expectancy even for nephews and nieces of schizophrenics is still as high as 3.7 per cent.

Eugenically most undesirable are the marriages of germinally affected brothers, sisters, half-brothers and half-sisters of schizophrenics with such partners as those who either obviously manifest certain symptoms of a schizophrenic trait or can be proved to have descended from a family tainted with schizophrenia. In these cases, the probability of the recurrence of schizophrenic psychoses in the offspring is so great that such marriages, if permitted at all, should at least be childless. (p. 131)

Moreover,

The partner in marriage of a schizophrenic patient should be prevented from remarrying during the period of fertility if any child of the first marriage is schizophrenic or suspected of schizophrenia. In this case, even if the individual in question gives no phenotypical signs of a predisposition to schizophrenia and plans a second marriage with a normal mate, the schizophrenic taint is present and would be transmitted to the children of the second marriage. (p. 131)

These glimpses of Kallmann's state of mind give us good reason to be profoundly suspicious that his data may be poisoned at the source by unrecognized biases, and that such biases might operate equally in the transmutation of data to "findings."

Kallmann is nothing if not a culturist and humanitarian. Let us see if we can disentangle from all this Kallmann the "scientist."

Kallmann bases his Berlin study on the records of a state mental hospital in the first ten years of its existence, from 1893 to 1902.

The original material which is the basis of our genetic and reproductive survey comprises 1,087 schizophrenic proband cases. This figure corresponds to the total number of schizophrenic case-histories still available in the archives of the Herzberge Hospital of Berlin from the first ten years of its existence (1893–1902). Thus, *it represents a random group untouched by any selective process.* (italics mine) (p. 7)

". . . sole criteria for selection" were that

1. The probands must have been committed to the Herzberge Hospital during the years from 1893–1902.
2. They must have been schizophrenics beyond the possibility of doubt, and the disease must have become manifest before the age of forty.

It hardly needs arguing that this state mental hospital population can by no means have been a representative sample of Berlin schizophrenics. It has recently been pointed out that selective processes work to bias the sample even of the mental hospital population itself (Rosenthal, 1961).

What makes for even greater difficulties is that only 251 (23.1 percent) of his probands (and equivalent percentages for various groups of relatives) were still alive at the time of his study (p. 28).

Diagnostic Procedure

Kallman goes into considerable detail to establish that his diagnosis of schizophrenia in the proband material is uninfluenced by knowledge of presence or absence of schizophrenia in relatives. He does not, however, attempt to diagnose the relatives uninfluenced by his knowledge of presence or absence of schizophrenia in probands. At no time has he submitted his data to the method of reciprocal blind diagnosis.

A crucial factor for the reliability and validity of his method is his *criterion* for his diagnosis, both of probands and of their relatives. At no time in his work does Kallmann give us a simple clear clinical description of the criteria for diagnosis of schizophrenia. The same is true of Siater. Kallmann indeed repudiates the possibility of purely objective clinical criteria of diagnosis, and even more remarkable, he repudiates any obligation to use the same criteria for the diagnosis of schizophrenia in his two groups, probands and relatives.

Thus his diagnosis of schizophrenia is an accordion one, it expands and contracts under his hands.

As Kallman says, in his secondary cases (i.e. relatives), ". . . *the diagnosis cannot be interpreted as narrowly as in the selection of our original proband cases*, where the avoidance of erroneous diagnoses was absolutely compulsory. . . ." (italics mine) (p. 101)

Apparently the avoidance of erroneous diagnosis is not so compulsory in the secondary cases (i.e. relatives). Besides, the accuracy of diagnosis "depends," he tells us,

> . . . much more on whether psychopathologic attributes are correctly interpreted, and evaluated in proper technical terms, than on whether the right final diagnosis is deduced from the sum of the identified symptoms. (pp. 101–102)

We have already seen the vituperative language Kallmann employs when he writes of schizophrenics. One must not forget that this language is not a language of conscious intentional abuse, employed in occasional asides. It is the very technical vocabulary which is his instrument for the scientific description of his primary data.

Here is how he brings a few of his "proper technical terms" into play in his description of his schizoid borderline cases.

> . . . the cranks and eccentrics suggesting schizophrenia, and all psychopathic types with schizoid personality— that is, stubborn and perverse recalcitrants, malicious and cold-hearted despots, superstitious and pietistic religio-maniacs, secretive recluses, sectarian dreamers out of touch with reality, and the over-pedantic, avaricious and literal-minded people. (p. 37)

And here is part of his "description" of his psychopathic borderline cases.

> In classifying the *schizoid psychopaths*, we again interpreted the diagnosis as strictly as possible, but did not make any further sub-division, such as we made for the different forms of schizophrenia. Our concept of schizoid psychopaths therefore embraces the unsociable, cold-hearted, indecisive and fanatic types regarded by Schneider as prototypes of the catanoid, heboid, schizoid and paranoid cases, respectively, as well as Hoffmann's bull-headed oafs, malicious tyrants, queer cranks, over-pedantic schemers, prudish "model children" and day-dreamers out of all touch with reality. However, we

included only psychopathic individuals who showed the fundamental schizoid characteristics of autistic introversion, emotional inadequacy, sudden surges of temperament and inappropriate motor response to emotional stimuli, and in whom such symptoms of schizoid abnormality as bigotry, pietism, avarice, superstition, suspicion, obstinacy or crankiness, were present to a striking and disproportionate degree. (pp. 102–103)

Is this anything else than a vocabulary of vituperation and denigration? But this is precisely his technical filter, his "proper technical terms" for correct interpretation and evaluation.

I for one find it impossible to penetrate through this verbal morass that is Kallmann's effort at interpretation and evaluation in proper technical terms to any identifiable symptoms. The passage serves well enough, however, as a basis for the evaluation of Kallmann. Yet there is no doubt about his scrupulosity in his own realm of total fictions.

We have already emphasized that we are still frequently unable to decide absolutely whether an eccentric borderline case is a homozygotic carrier of the predisposition to schizophrenia with inhibited manifestation, or the most definite type of a germinally affected taint-carrier, or perhaps only a "symptomatic" schizoid type without direct connection to the heredity-circle of schizophrenia. It may also be probable that a certain percentage of germinally affected carriers of the predisposition to schizophrenia escape discovery under the equally vague concept of psychological "normality." (p. 103)

This reminds one of nothing so much as those debates of medieval Schoolmen concerning the vexed question of the number of angels that could stand together on the head of a needle. Kallmann cuts himself fatefully adrift from any obligation to the world of empirical experience.

Since the "right final diagnosis" depends more on interpretation and evaluation in "proper technical terms" than on the sum of identified symptoms, ". . . in the last analysis the accurate recognition and appraisal of schizophrenic manifestations must depend on the subjective delicacy of touch and personal ability of the individual investigator" (p. 102).

Schizophrenia is, for Kallmann, an endogenous psychosis. It is an endogenous psychosis of genetic origin. But only a psychosis that appears to him to be an endogenous psychosis is truly schizophrenic.

Since it appears that not clinical signs and symptoms but Kallman's subjective delicacy of touch is the criterion of the "endogenous" nature of a psychosis, we, lacking the special delicacy of touch possessed by Kallmann, remain outside his arcana. Very seldom are we given any hints that can allow us any glimpse of those variables that are crucial to us.

> 6. John R., born 1892; had no trade; was unmarried and childless; in 1935 still a patient in the Herzberge Hospital. He received a college preparatory education but then remained at home with his mother. In 1920 the police took his mother and himself to the Herzberge Hospital (readmission for his mother), as both had become completely demented. They found him naked in a room where his mother had kept him locked up for years, "to keep him out of the hands of their enemies." On admission to the hospital he was already in an advanced stage of schizophrenic dementia. He appeared dazed and apathetic, murmured unintelligibly to himself, and refused to answer questions. He laughed without apparent reason, stared at the ceiling and was incontinent of urine and feces. (Hebephrenia). (p. 166)

On this data we are expected to be able to diagnose, with Kallmann, two separate psychoses of endogenous origin passed on from mother to son through the "genes." One wonders what an "exogenous" psychotic process is for Kallman, until one realizes that "exogenous" means for him physical traumata and toxins. Kallmann's grasp of the nature of the effects people have on each other is totally primitive.

Kallmann justifies his diagnosis (a) by his exercise of this

"subjective delicacy of touch," (b) with the already diagnosed proband in full view, (c) with an admitted double
standard (one for probands, one for relatives), by under-
taking to describe each family individually and in such detail that "these descriptions will facilitate a check on our
diagnostic tenets at any time." However, Kallmann appears
not to know what an objective description is (see further
below); and, further, his conclusions are based to only a
very limited extent on those cases per se. The descriptions
he gives simply show that in ninety-two families, various
cases of schizophrenia occur. There is no dispute about
that, nor can any conclusion be drawn from it.

A note on his "correction of figures." One remembers that
his data is based on archives for the years 1892 to 1903—
1,087 cases, 231 probands living. Of the 2,000 children of
these probands 797 were living. How many probands *and*
their children are dead, we do not know.

Of these 2,000 children of probands, he finds 92 definite
cases of schizophrenia, and 16 doubtful cases. These are
the cases he describes clinically. From this raw figure of 92
out of 2,000 or 4.6 percent, by the addition of doubtful
cases and various "corrections," he ends up with a calculated expectancy rate of 16.4 percent for the total undif-
ferentiated group of proband children.

Since 1938, Kallmann has confined himself to the presentation of tables[2] and figures, to restatements of his theory,
larded with continued polemics against doubting Thom-
ases, and the occasional presentation of anecdotal cases.
The diagnostic aspects of this later work are not revealed
to us in detail, but they appear to be based on the same
principles as his earlier work.

After settling in New York (1937), Kallmann developed
"the twin-family method" in order to demonstrate further

[2] The main presentation of his figures is given in papers from
1946, 1950, 1952, and 1956.

the genetic theory of schizophrenia. His program has been based on the following argument.

In order to substantiate [the genetic] theory, geneticists have to demonstrate that the tendency to develop a severe psychosis increases in proportion to the degree of blood relationship to a family member showing the given type of psychosis, since organic inheritance cannot operate without the factor of blood relationship. Another requirement would be that it is the incidence of schizophrenia, rather than that of a manic-depressive or another type of psychosis, which is apt to be increased in the blood relatives of schizophrenic index cases, and vice versa. (1952, p. 284)

In his years as an investigator, a compiler of figures, and as a writer, Kallmann has become more sophisticated than in his early days.

His endeavor has been to produce sliding scales of specific morbidity rates correlated with degrees of consanguinity (from monozygotic twins and dizygotic twins to full sibs, half sibs, cousins, half-cousins, etc.). These tables show sliding scales that can be correlated to degrees of consanguinity.

It seems that a diagnosis of schizophrenia is likely to be made in about one percent of the general population; Kallmann's corrected figures are as follows:

. . . the children of one schizophrenic parent have a probability of developing the disease nineteen times that of the general population. The grandchildren and the nephews and nieces are about five times more likely to show a recurrence of schizophrenia than is the average person. The schizophrenia rate of the parents of schizophrenics approximated 10 per cent. The expectancy for brothers and sisters as well as for the fraternal twin partners of schizophrenics is somewhere around 14 per cent., while that for half-siblings of schizophrenics is about 7 per cent., and that for step-siblings, 1.8 per cent. The highest morbidity rates are found among the children of two schizophrenic parents, who have about

eighty times the average expectancy, and among the
identical twin partners of schizophrenic index cases, who
show an expectancy rate of 85 per cent. (1948, p. 252)

These estimated variations in the schizophrenia rate

> . . . are correlated with *different degrees of consan-*
> *guinity* to a schizophrenic index case, but not with simi-
> larity or dissimilarity in the respective *environments* of
> the twin partners and other siblings of schizophrenics.
> About one quarter of one-egg twin pairs show con-
> cordance as to schizophrenia without similar environ-
> ment, while close to one-half of two-egg twin pairs
> remain discordant, even if the two twins have been ex-
> posed to precisely the same environment. This observa-
> tion excludes the possibility of explaining the difference
> in morbidity between one-egg and two-egg co-twins on
> non-genetic grounds, that is, by a simple correlation be-
> tween closeness of blood relationship and increasing
> similarity in environment. (p. 253)

Kallmann has by now established a diagnostic procedure
that cannot lose, and he has ample room for appropriate
"corrections": in so many families the twin or co-twin is
dead, in so many the parents are dead, in so many the
history is "insufficient."

He has also become the *only investigator in the world,*
so far as I know, who finds absolutely no manic-depressive
psychoses in the monozygotic co-twins of his schizophrenic
index cases. And furthermore, his sample (1952)

> . . . included neither a dizygotic pair with a schizo-
> phrenic psychosis in one member and a manic-depres-
> sive psychosis in the other, nor a single manic-depressive
> index family with an *authentic case* of schizophrenia
> among the parents and siblings of the index cases. (ital-
> ics mine) (p. 286)

The sixty-four thousand dollar question is, what is an
"authentic" case?

Since Kallmann claims the right in principle not only to
ascribe a schizophrenic phenotype to a nonschizophrenic

genotype, but to ascribe a nonschizophrenic phenotype to a schizophrenic genotype, according to the "subjective delicacy" of his own judgment, his finding is perhaps less surprising than it would otherwise be.

The decision as to when a person is an "authentic case" or not appears to be taken by Kallmann with full knowledge of the symptoms of other members of the family. He has never made this crucial part of his work public, but he has laid down his principles clearly enough.

> Cases which present a schizophrenic picture clinically but lack the hereditary predisposition, must be excluded from the disease group of "genuine" schizophrenia and differentiated as "schizoform" psychoses of exogenous origin. (1938, p. 26)

If schizophrenic, then a priori, hereditary predisposition. If no hereditary predisposition, then a priori not schizophrenic. If two blood relatives develop schizophreniform psychoses, this proves that they are suffering from "endogenous psychoses, genetically determined."

A leading human geneticist has argued the other way.

> It lies in the nature of twin studies that *the existence of nongenetic factors in mental disease,* as in other traits, is proven beyond doubt whenever discordant identical pairs are encountered, but that the existence of genetic factors is not *unequivocally established* when the twins are concordant. (Stern, 1960, p. 581)

The So-Called Controlled Experiment of Nature— Twin Studies

It is generally held to be the case that nature has provided two control experiments, and that "the results" of both support the genetic hypothesis, since (*a*) monovular twins brought up in "the same" environment as dizygotic twins show a higher concordance rate for schizophrenia than do dizygotics brought up together, and (*b*) monozy-

gotic twins brought up separately are still highly concordant for schizophrenia.

Kallmann's extensive twin studies are presented in the
form of tables of percentages of "concordance," with an
occasional anecdotal reference to a case, or part of a case.

He introduced the categories of separated and nonsepa-
rated twins in his 1946 study. Separated means, "separated
for five years or more prior to the onset of schizophrenia in
the index twin." "The separated concordant twins had lived
apart for an average of 11.8 years before disease onset in
the first twin, and the discordant index pairs had reached
a total average age of 33 years." (1946, p. 317).

Elsewhere he states that

> . . . our group of separated one-egg pairs include twins
> who developed schizophrenia at almost the same time,
> although their separation took place soon after birth and
> led to apparently very different life conditions. (1946,
> p. 316)

In view of the fact that such findings would, in the
geneticists view, be very strong evidence for their theory,
it is surprising that *Kallmann has not seen fit to present any
case histories of such allegedly concordant uniovular pairs
separated "soon after birth"* since 1938, when he presented
what in his view was one such case.

The world literature on monozygotic twins with reference to schizophrenia has recently been effectively re-
viewed by Jackson (1960). Jackson points out that it is not
generally realized that there are only two reported cases of
monozygotic twins, allegedly concordant for schizophrenia,
who have been separated within the first year of life (Kallmann, 1938, Craike and Slater, 1945).

I propose to examine the data presented in these two
cases in some detail. One can then compare this data
against the claims made on its behalf by the geneticists.
Moreover, since the authors attach crucial importance to
them, these cases are presented in more detail than any of
their other cases. We can reasonably assume that presenta-

tion and critical assessment of data are intended as models of their kind.

THE TWINS KAETE AND LISA—KALLMANN (1938)

This case is presented by Kallmann as

> . . . a pair of positively identical and definitely schizophrenic twins. . . . the case illustrates, almost as clearly as a laboratory experiment in breeding, the importance of constitutional and dispositional factors in the manifestation of identical hereditary predisposition to schizophrenia, and is undoubtedly unique. (p. 207)

He believes that these twins

> . . . definitely refute the theory that schizophrenic psychosis of twins is principally conditioned by such similar environmental influences as are usually present in histories involving twins and are therefore often cited as the only causative factors. *More pertinent evidence than is offered here for the hereditary conditioning of schizophrenia will not readily be forthcoming.* (italics mine) (p. 210)

Briefly, these two sisters were the illegitimate offspring of a domestic servant, who bore them in hospital but one day went out and never returned.

> She lived for a while on charity and on small contributions from her brothers, until she developed a pulmonary tuberculosis. From then on, she very rapidly deteriorated physically and psychically, and died at the age of 43, in the Buch Hospital, of tuberculous spondylitis. (p. 208)

The twins' maternal grandmother is described as a severe alcoholic who died "in delirium" at the age of forty-two. Their mother had four brothers. One unmarried brother died after a lifelong career of drunkenness. Three other brothers, married, without children, were described as "eccentric borderline cases."

Two of these eccentric brothers lived in different cities

and were on bad terms with each other. Kaete went to live with one, Lisa with the other (Kallmann does not say when). Until they were ten they lived apart, but saw each other a few times briefly. Later they met more frequently and subsequently developed a reciprocal antagonism to each other.

Kallmann does not say who supplied the histories of either Kaete or Lisa (presumably their reciprocally antagonistic, eccentric borderline uncles and/or their wives), but he records without reservation that ". . . *despite different environments in every aspect, the twins had a similar development in point of character and social experience*" (italics mine) (p. 208).

As far as we are given any information at all, we are led to suppose that they grew up in environments that were mirror images of each other. By "different environments" Kallmann perhaps means that they lived in different towns, walked in different streets. What did these childless aunts think of these girls and their mother? Were the twins both told that their mother was a bad lot? Did they each grow up under the shadow that they would take after her? Were they both given to understand how grateful they ought to be for what had been done for them? At any event, the different uncles or their wives appear to have developed identical attributions about the twins. Both are said to have been "problem children, difficult to teach, stubborn, callous and indifferent" and although "they advanced in their different public schools to the upper grades, their refractory conduct reduced the foster-parents on both sides to the verge of despair, and gradually reached such a depth [!] that both girls were always doing the opposite of what they were told." The common language used to describe both may indicate that they were both "the same," and/or that their uncles and their wives regarded them and treated them in the same way.

After they left school, Kaete found employment in a factory, and Lisa became a domestic servant. At this point their life-curves diverged sharply for a few years. While Lisa remained in the well-protected shelter of a private family, Kaete, at the age of fifteen, was seduced by a fellow-worker in the factory. Four months before her sixteenth birthday, she gave birth to a baby, which was raised in an orphanage and has as yet developed normally. (pp. 208–209)

After the birth of this baby Kaete became anxious, perturbed, and excited.

> She lapsed very quickly into a profound catatonic stupor, which led, in October, 1928, to her commitment to the Herzberge Hospital, and continued, with little change, for over a year. In November, 1929, she gradually became more relaxed and approachable and a month later it was possible to discharge her under family care. However, the improvement was of relatively brief duration. From February, 1930, on, her condition grew worse and worse. (p. 209)

For some reason, in February 1930 also, Lisa (who until then had apparently not been "ill" in any way) now became slowly and increasingly more and more helpless and emotionally indifferent, until in June she joined her sister in the Herzberge Hospital. "She has never been quite so ill as Kaete" and

> Even if Lisa's episodes of excitement have followed exactly the same course as Kaete's, they have been shorter, and the intervals longer. During the last year of our observation, Lisa presented merely the picture of a schizophrenic defect and even in her worst stages was quite far from that level of mental deterioration which Kaete had reached. (p. 209)

This case "proves," according to Kallmann,

> . . . that definite somatogenic factors must count as *dispositional* determinants in the manifestation of a hereditary predisposition to schizophrenia. The fact that one of the identical twins developed schizophrenia immediately after child-bearing and almost two years ear-

lier than the other twin, who did not undergo pregnancy, can hardly be interpreted as coincidence. It is rather to be regarded as proof that the reason for such acceleration of the disease onset must be sought in certain somatic processes instigated by pregnancy, and furthering the manifestation of the individual taint. (p. 210)

In his subsequent studies of twins Kallmann does not give any case histories even as "adequate" as the above. When one sees, however, his continued completely uncritical and naïve approach to his data, there is no indication that his assertions about "completely different environments" are any less naïve; nor that he has more grasp of the pitfalls of retrospective data, or of reports from family members that may be equally biased due to fantasies held in common (these stubborn, callous children who descended to such a depth that they wouldn't do what they were told). One can place no more confidence in Kallmann's assessments of "concordance" of "environment" than in those of life history and diagnosis.

Folie à Deux in Uniovular Twins Reared Apart[3]

In 1945 an extraordinary paper appeared in the leading British neurological journal, purporting to be an account of identical twins concordant for schizophrenia and brought up separately.

[3] Craike and Slater (1945). The title is itself sufficiently misleading, since "folie à deux" is by definition a supposed psychosis of association, whereas the thesis of the authors is that no such factor enters into the etiology of their "illness." The twins each involved the other in their suspicions and it is this mutual involvement in a paranoid psychosis system which suggested the title of "folie à deux," although the possibility that the psychosis of either "induced" that of the other, has, we think to be rejected.

This is to say: we are calling two skin rashes mutually contagious rashes but we are writing a paper to show that they are not contagious. Folie à deux has never been used to characterize people living apart who have delusions about each other.

Craike and Slater claim a great deal for the significance of this study. Identical twins reared apart are very rare.

After intensive search extending over many years, Newman, Freeman and Holzinger were only able to discover in the whole of the U.S.A. nineteen such pairs. . . . None of their pairs had any mental illness, and, as far as we know, the case here reported is unique in the literature. (p. 213)

Actually, the case of the identical twins Kaete and Lisa (above) was reported by Kallmann in 1938.

The authors summarize their findings as follows.

Two uniovular twins of 52 are described, who were separated at the age of 9 months, but each in due course developed a paranoid psychosis. Concordance of childhood neurosis, of life story, of personality, and of eventual symptomatology are shown, despite very different upbringings. The principal difference between the psychoses is that while one shows a chronic insidiously progressive paranoia, the other shows paranoid symptoms only episodically. Each sister centres her delusions around the other: this appears in one of them to be reactive to the accusations of the other. Both are regarded as being the subjects of a basically schizophrenic illness. (pp. 220–221)

It is very difficult indeed to find any plausible theory to account for how Craike and Slater arrive at these conclusions, on the basis of the evidence they bring forward. Apart from the age of the twins and the fact that they were separated at nine months, not one of their conclusions is supported by their evidence, and much of it is directly contradicted.

The simplest way to demonstrate this is to compare the lives of these twins in two tables.

FLORENCE

Age   Florence born 1893.
             Brother—five years older.

9 months   Mother died. Brought up by maternal aunt—
"made her home with her until her death in
1944 aged 85" (but see work record). Very
happy with her. Her childhood was happy
"although rather nervous and frightened of
the dark." She did not walk in her sleep; had
no nightmares.

Ordinary elementary school, rather backward—reached Standard IV. Missed a lot of
schooling due to fainting attacks, but picked
up a lot later from reading. Left school at 14.

14 years   Children's nursemaid. Took some of her
employer's soap—charged with theft and put
in a convent for two years. "While there she
was happy." Ever since she has worked as a
domestic head housemaid—regular employment. Stayed with her aunt in intervals between jobs.

18   "Nervous debility"—abdominal pain, vomiting and nervousness. Went to stay with
another aunt and recovered. Apart from this
no nervous trouble in the past.
Describes herself as quiet but cheerful, always much the same mood. Very religious in
youth.
In 1916 an aunt died leaving money to
Florence and Edith. Solicitor got in touch
with them.

24   Met Edith for first time. Noticed how alike
they were—rather took a fancy to Edith.
Met twice more, then letters from Edith accusing her of spying. A fellow servant said
"You think a lot of yourself, but you've been
to prison." Thinks it was through Edith that
knowledge of her past theft got around.

Edith wrote: "Why do you come down on the back of Alf's bike spying on me? I know it's you because of your lemon hat and brown coat."

No more trouble until years later, then: "People said they knew all about me. They (the staff) said, 'Why don't you get married? That's what's the matter with you.'" "There was a general undercurrent."

50 Met Edith again. "We spent one or two nice weekends. I mentioned I had a chance of two rooms and should we take them. She said no, she wanted me to keep away. She accused me that Sunday of going to neighbours saying she was mental." (Informant: Florence)

51 *27.12.44:* "Admitted. Physically n.a.d. Mentally very depressed, weeps and sobs copiously as she tells of all the undercurrent against her. People say she is mad, she is mental, they throw up at her all her past life. She is determined to get at the bottom of it. Only once did she actually catch a voice, a man's voice, saying horrible things."

29.12.44: "Seen by magistrate. Continues to complain of some undercurrent going on against her."

6.1.45: "Improved, still some depression but not so worried by delusional ideas. Seen by Dr. Walker who notes: depressed and preoccupied, although she says she feels much happier under care. Only one remark has been passed about her since admission, but there were plenty before. . . . She says that among other things the voices have told her that she is mental, they have accused her of having been in prison." (from notes)

EDITH

Age	Edith born 1893.
	Brother—five years older.
9 months	Mother died. Stayed on with father. Led a miserable childhood. Walked in her sleep before her first confession, which she dreaded. Had nightmares of being flogged.
8½ years	Father very violent, drank heavily. Sent to children's home, where she stayed until she was 19.
	Did quite well at school, reaching top Standard (VII).
15½	Left school.
	Farm work. "Nervous dyspepsia and anemia."
	Knew of Florence—never met—never corresponded. Florence made trouble by writing to father telling him Edith told her he was a drunkard.
20	Cardiff Workhouse. Father took her home, but soon told her to get out. Ran away to live with an uncle.
	Came to London from Wales to seek employment. Says her uncle paid her fare, but that Florence says that she (Florence) paid it, and that Edith is under an obligation to her.
24	Met Florence for first time (money left them by aunt who had died the year before, and solicitor contacted them).
	Says Florence accused her of stealing ten shillings from her purse. Edith denies this, but says she stole from her father when living with him.

She and Florence saw a little of each other but could not get on. She says Florence used to spy on her and write anonymous letters to employers.

She saw Florence in the street on a bicycle with a man, recognized her because she was wearing a yellow hat, and knew she was spying on her.

47   Continued living in London, worked as a domestic. Excellent references. Quiet, reserved, few friends, hardworking, stable mood, keenly religious (Anglo-Catholic).

Last employer states he dismissed her because of "delusionary ideas"—*being accused of wrongdoing*—but honest, willing, trustworthy, kindly. The sisters did not see much of each other, never agreed. Edith always said Florence only called for financial help.

Directed to Glass factory.

Welfare Officer says she is very good at her work, seems quite happy there, but has suggested she would like her release to become a nun. "The only odd thing about her is that she asks to see Welfare Officer from time to time, and inquires whether people are talking about her and whether she is causing any trouble."

52   Edith says she saw Florence watching her house. She thinks Florence must be jealous. She has had a very hard struggle, everybody has been against her, and she has lost many good jobs in domestic service. All this is entirely due to the influence of Florence.

On 8.1.45 Florence was examined: the report was that affective rapport was good, there was no evidence of any shallowness of affect or any bizarre quality, nor of any schizophrenic features of attitude, expression, or motor behavior. She did not appear to be hallucinated. Intellectually she was well preserved.

By 29.1.45 she was back at work and feeling very well.

Edith seen later, not in hospital, was suspicious and reserved but "there were no characteristic schizophrenic symptoms. Intellectually she was well preserved, but probably of low average intelligence."

Diagnosis. From the data presented it appears likely that Florence had a depressive reaction following the death of her aunt. This cleared up *within one month*, with at no time any evidence whatever in her life history, during her breakdown, or after, of any signs or symptoms that could justify a diagnosis of schizophrenia.

A history of chronic ideas of reference are no grounds for a diagnosis of schizophrenia in a fifty-two-year-old woman who shows no schizophrenic symptoms on examination or other schizophrenic traits in her life history. The "undercurrents" are of the typical depressive kind ("Why haven't you got married?," "You were in prison," etc.).

Edith also is somewhat depressed, apparently with a tendency to attribute dissatisfaction with, or criticisms of, herself to others, and to blame this on Florence.

Neither shows any insidious development. Edith, so far from deteriorating, held her last job for eleven years. Her employers are happy with her in her present job, which she has held for four years. She goes to the Welfare Officer from time to time to be reassured that she is not causing any trouble.

But consider the way all this is built up by the authors:

Note the linguistic tricks used to establish concordances —e.g. the evidence for concordance in respect of "childhood neurosis" is presented thus: "Both were nervous as children; Edith walked in her sleep and had nightmares, Florence had fainting attacks and was nervous of the dark" (p. 219).

Equally this could be written: Edith walked in her sleep, Florence did not. Edith had nightmares, Florence did not. Florence had fainting attacks, Edith did not.

Equally ridiculous is the way concordance for life story is built up—e.g. Florence had a stable home, an "affectionate" (what does this mean?) maternal aunt and has lived with her all her life until a year ago, we are told: *but* she had regular employment and stayed with her only between jobs. When she was ill at 18 she went to stay with another aunt, and there got better. "Both stole as children or adolescents, Edith from her father, Florence from her employer" [a bar of soap!] (p. 219).

To rate them concordant for "personality" (as they do) on the basis of such evidence is to reduce psychiatry to the level of the historical reasoning of *1066 and All That.* "James I slobbered at the mouth and had favourites, he was thus a Bad King." Besides, the story of a fifty-two-year-old unmarried domestic servant, gathered from her in the midst of what seems like a reactive depression in the involutional period, that she was put away for two years in a nunnery when she was eighteen for stealing soap from her employer, should be treated with considerable reserve (as far as factual history is concerned).

"Their careers bear very striking resemblances." But they do not seem to resemble each other more than might the careers of any two domestic servants.

The "pièce de résistance" is the concordance for psychiatric diagnosis. As they rightly say in their paper, the authors have "no positive evidence" to support a diagnosis of schizophrenia. However, by the time it comes to their summary we are told that there *is* concordance in all respects, and that each "in due course" developed a paranoid psychosis.

What is first mentioned as the "paranoid state" of Edith later becomes "a chronic insidiously progressive paranoia" (!!), and finally "both are regarded as being the subjects of a basically schizophrenic illness."

The reasoning here is the reasoning of a witch trial. It is clear that if you are "basically" schizophrenic on an a priori basis there is not much you can do to disprove it. You may establish good rapport, have friends (note the verbal trick: a basically schizophrenic person will have "few friends"; a "normal" person may have "a few friends"), do your work in an ordinary way, show no affective impoverishment, splitting, disorder of verbal or motor behavior, not be hallucinated, and develop a perfectly usual type of reactive depression with paranoid features, but you are "basically schizophrenic." And if you are the monozygotic twin of a "basically schizophrenic" propositus then the diagnosis is almost sealed. No matter that you are a slightly deaf spinster of fifty-two whose mother died (nine months), who was beaten by your violent drunken father (and still have the mark of his razor on your forehead) who later remarried and sent you to a home (eight and a half), from which (although you were apparently bright at school) you were sent to work on a farm, and when you became run down you were sent to a workhouse, etc., no matter that since then you have had good jobs and only two changes in the last fifteen years—if you feel you've had a hard struggle, and mistrust your sister and others, then you are suffering from a "chronic insidiously progressive paranoia" and are "basically schizophrenic" into the bargain!

It is on the basis of such evidence that we are informed we have now "no reason but lack of open-mindedness" (Slater) to refuse to accept as proven beyond all reasonable doubt the genetic theory of schizophrenia.

These cases, Kaete and Lisa and Lily and Mary (below) are the only two such alleged cases in the world literature.

THE WORK OF SLATER

Slater's main work on twins and schizophrenia is based on the 297 pairs of twins whose propositi were gleaned from the records of ten mental hospitals (1953).

Slater divided the propositi and co-twins into five diagnostic categories: schizophrenic; affective illness; psychopathic and neurotic; organic; normal. He established uniovularity and binovularity. He then rated the co-twin as concordant or discordant in terms of his five categories.

Twins with schizophrenic propositus. Slater has forty-one such uniovular pairs, twenty-eight of which he estimates to be concordant. Of these twenty-eight, however, he states (p. 55) that there is "gross insufficiency of information in three cases (*4, 118, 41, 134* and *104, 146*), and there are disputable qualities about two cases (*14, 123* and *20, 127*). He goes on, however, to state that "*it would seem captious to exclude them, as in every case schizophrenia is much more probable than normality or any other diagnosis*" (italics mine).

When we examine these and others of his cases, we see how truly extraordinary this reasoning is. The following are some examples of his diagnostic methods.

4 (p. 118)   Fanny   (schizophrenic concordant
                 xEileen   uniovular group)

Informants: Fanny
                 Fanny's daughter-in-law

1. Daughter-in-law had not heard of Fanny's mental illness.

2. Neither her family nor the neighbors had noticed anything odd about her.

3. Fanny "suppressed" all mention of her own mental illness.

4. "Fact" obtained from history of her twin sister given at the time of her admission to hospital (1899).

5. "No sign of schizophrenic symptoms on examination of Fanny."

6. In short, "no facts obtainable about the nature of her past mental illness, but the probabilities are very greatly in favor of it having been a schizophrenic one."

Slater's diagnosis for Fanny: schizophrenia.

Concordant Uniovular Group. 20   *117* (p. 154)   xHilda
                                                      Mary

Informant: Hilda's husband.
Evidence in respect of Mary:

At 29 Mary married a railway clerk in a responsible
position and they had a good home and nothing to worry
about, though Mary continued to do so. She developed
a large goitre in the forties and in July 1936, aged 43,
her behaviour became peculiar. On one occasion she
visited her sister (informant) and knocked on the door;
but when the sister put her head out of the window she
saw Mary running up the street. At last on a Friday
Mary became acutely ill mentally and on the following
Wednesday died of "bronchitis and melancholia." No
clinical record can be traced. (p. 155)

The nature of Mary's illness is quite unclear, as she died
before characteristic signs could be seen: *although most
probably schizophrenia,* her illness could be regarded
as a symptomatic psychosis coming on in an abnormal
personality. Hilda's illness is unquestionably schizophrenic. The role played by goitre in both twins is unclear. (italics mine) (p. 156)

5   20   (p. 127)   Lilian
                        Mary

Mary had certain "paranoid ideas" (that men are in love
with her) at menopause. Now a deaf old maid living with
her deaf sister, these ideas have largely evaporated as the
years went on.

9   41   (p. 134)   Daisy
                        xChristine

Daisy:

Age 27: nervous breakdown—could not concentrate,
could not work, confused, thought she would go mad.

Age 33: husband killed while she was in maternity hospital after birth of third child, she developed mental symptoms, was in a mental hospital for a year. She has since remarried.

Examined in 1948 she was unwilling to give details, but
said she suffered badly from nerves. From the conditions
in which she was living, it seemed probable that she had
deteriorated socially [??].

I.e. Daisy: two illnesses—27 and 33.

"Seems probable that they, too, were schizophrenic, from the affectively impaired state they left behind."

I can find *no evidence in either case of schizophrenia.*

If there seems to be "affectively impaired state" (one of the most unreliable of impressions, especially in old people), this is held to be evidence that a previous unattested illness was most probably schizophrenia. However, if (as 198, 199, p. 168) "Nothing particularly schizophrenic was observed, and affect seemed normal," a psychiatric opinion, that would be reversed if it seemed improbable on genetic grounds, is accepted on flimsy clinical evidence.

That is, *lack* of "impairment" is not used unbiasedly *contra*-schizophrenia when concordance is "probable" on genetic grounds.

In 9, 41, "affective impairment" is used as an index of past schizophrenia: in 24, 25 (p. 166) lack of affective impairment is used as an index of good recovery.[4]

Schizophrenia only becomes "more probable than normality or any other diagnosis" to Slater because he is convinced that the uniovular twin of a schizophrenic propositus is much more probably schizophrenic than not. Since this is the hypothesis he is testing, one is surprised that it is also his initial assumption. So strong is this assumption that Slater does not hesitate to invent the *diagnosis*, even in the *total* absence of any information whatever about the nature of the alleged illness in the co-twin, even, indeed, in the presence of doubt as to existence of any mental illness (4, 118).

Slater manipulates his diagnostic categories in various ways, on the basis not of empirical evidence, but of his presuppositions.

The following are some of the tactics used by Slater to *invent* the concordances that he "discovers."

[4] From our own research. In one committal form the following was offered as evidence of insanity: "Patient denies hearing the voice of God on the telephone."

1. *The chameleon method.* Schizophrenia for Slater is a chameleon. He ensures himself against the need for consistency in his criteria for diagnosis by not defining any phenomenological or clinical criteria. The same clinical features can at one time be evidence for schizophrenia, at other times, evidence against schizophrenia (e.g. p. 275).

2. *The circular method.* He is far ever from diagnosing a co-twin "blindly" without reference to the diagnosis of the other twin. He appears to believe, like Kallmann, that the statistical concordance that he thereby achieves raises the validity of his individual diagnosis. As the diagnosis in each case is made on the basis that the closer the blood relationship to a diagnosed schizophrenic, the higher the probability of schizophrenia in the co-twin, he creates his own concordance figures by his own assumptions.

3. *The accordion method.* Schizophrenia for Slater, as for Kallmann, is an *accordion diagnosis.* It expands and contracts in range of symptomatology in accordance with its a priori antecedent probability. Once more, he cannot but arrive at figures that reflect *but in no way validate* his own preconceptions.

The above three fallacies are *fallacies of validation.* It does not follow that Slater's diagnoses are necessarily *unreliable.* That is, another psychiatrist, or a whole generation of psychiatrists, sharing his preconceptions, and committing the same methodological errors, as they are trained to do, may well arrive at the same diagnosis.

The heart of the matter is quite simple. If Slater wishes to show that concordance is high in uniovular twins he cannot justifiably use his knowledge of their uniovularity in order to make a diagnosis of concordance. Only one method is permissible: to diagnose the co-twins blindly, independently either of (*a*) uniovularity or binovularity, or (*b*) diagnostic category of propositus or co-twin.

As it is, in many cases, the co-twin is diagnosed as schizophrenic because the propositus is, or as not schizophrenic because the propositus is not (e.g. in the affective group). The resulting figures, poisoned at the source, will reflect only Slater's a priori bias.

Slater's figures do not show empirical objective concordances, but the subjectively concordant expectations of Slater. This explains the fact that he indeed finds little else than his own diagnoses to be concordant: onset, symptomatology (with the limited exception of one subgroup), course, outcome are not simultaneously concordant, and on the whole they stick out as refractorily discordant. The full extent of the contamination of Slater's diagnoses only becomes apparent, however, when one has before one his treatment of his other groups of pairs.

To Slater it is improbable a priori that affective illness can occur in the identical co-twin of a schizophrenic, and also unlikely that it should occur in families where schizophrenia is the supposed genetic taint (the expectancy rate for affective illness in such families would be that of the population average). However, he conceives that it is not impossible for two separate taints to weave a contrapuntal pattern through the generations of the one family.

His procedure in this respect is once more to use his presupposition to bias his diagnoses, which, when added up, are then offered as evidence in support of his presupposition. Thus, if schizophrenia seems to Slater the plausible diagnosis on genetic grounds, then an illness beginning with affective signs and culminating in hallucinations and delusions is clearly only revealing its true schizophrenic nature. However, if the diagnosis of affective illness is the more plausible on genetic grounds(in view of the fact that this is the diagnosis of the propositus), then hallucinations and delusions will be only schizophreniform, mere "asylum artifacts" (162, 273).

Slater has of course every right sometimes to concur with, sometimes to dissent from, the opinion of other psychiatrists. What is suggested is that not purely clinical considerations move him to concur with another psychiatrist's diagnosis of schizophrenia when he himself finds no present signs of past schizophrenic defect, or to reverse a diagnosis of schizophrenia when clinical evidence seems to support it. Can one suppose he would have reversed the diagnosis in 162, if he had not known the diagnosis of the propositus?

Schizophrenia and affective illness, indeed, become more and more mystical in the worst connotations of this word. If a genotypical schizophrenia may present as a phenotypical depression, and a genotypical depression may be a phenotypical schizophrenia (p. 65), diagnosis must become an esoteric art practiced in a hermetic circle. It requires great "artistry" to diagnose an affective illness in a schizoid personality, or a schizophrenic illness in a cyclothymic personality. In the affective binovular concordant pairs, for instance, Fanny (173, 294) is a clear example of a twin who shows as many schizophrenic features as half the twins diagnosed as schizophrenic.

I have already noted how such mystifications are supported by the sustained use in particular life histories of jargon words that convey, to the properly attuned psychiatrist, the required inflection. This verbal induction of bias is far from straight clinical description, but it is more subtle than that practiced by Kallmann.

Consider, for instance, the account of two old ladies, Mary (20, 127), and Milly (105, 283), who are, of course, members of different twin pairs.

> Mary was seen at home by P.S.W. She too was very deaf. She willingly showed her visitor up the stairs, and in walking up had an odd way of bending her head and shoulders from side to side as she mounted each step, at the same time humming *monotonously* but vigorously (not realizing she could be heard). On learning the purpose of the visit she became *agitated,* and at the mention of finger-prints *suspected* her visitor came from the police. However, it was possible to soothe her, and even take the prints, and towards the end of the interview she was *jocular* and *playful* in a way reminiscent of the state of Lily as described by the doctor on her first admission to hospital. She spoke in exaggerated terms of her love affairs, of the number of which she was proud, and in a laughing, *excited* way of her many difficulties at work and changes of job at the time of the menopause. She had no insight into her state of mind at that time. (italics mine) (p. 128)

Milly was seen in 1936, but refused any physical examination. Mentally she appeared quite normal and was *perfectly cooperative apart from refusing* to have fingerprints taken, *etc.* A photograph taken of the twins together shows a remarkable facial resemblance and close similarity in stature and build. Both twins are of outstanding pyknic habitus. The only notable physical difference is that Milly is not deaf but Molly has recently become deaf and has had a discharge from one ear.

Milly, when visited again by P.S.W. in 1948, was as pleasing and cooperative as ever, but again refused to have fingerprints taken ("I'm very respectable"). She scorned the idea that she might be nervous and in manner was *friendly, good-humoured* and *downright*. She denied the idea that drink might be the cause of Molly's illness—"She might have one or two now and again, and when she does she likes to talk about it." (italics mine) (p. 285)

The identical twin who is a priori genotypically a Slater schizophrenic tends to be "jocular" rather than "good-humored," "rude" rather than "downright," "affectively impaired" rather than "dejected," "excited' rather than "elated," and so on: a "paranoid" feature will be played up in one, played down in another.

The practiced psychiatrist can readily predict Slater's diagnosis from his choice of vocabulary, but it would be difficult to make any independent diagnosis from the behavior itself. (Mary is rated schizophrenic, and Milly "affectively" ill.) Besides the inflected vocabulary, Mary's refusal to have her fingerprints taken is emphasized, while no significance is attached to Milly's refusal.

Another curious feature is Slater's estimation of concordance of "environment." The life histories of Maud and Marion (162, 273) are quite discordant. There is little clinical evidence for rating them both affective: perhaps Maud is somewhat hysterical and Marion somewhat schizophrenic. But to Slater they are *geno*typically similar, so Maud will have a genotypical affective illness presenting hysterical features, while Marion will have a genotypical affective illness that is atypically schizophreniform. *"But"*, says Slater, *"considering how different their environments were they are really remarkably concordant."*

> Difficulties of diagnosis are prominent in this case; nevertheless the author is inclined to regard Marion's illness as primarily affective, the paranoid features being secondary and explicable, in part at least, by her extremely isolated situation and the hopelessness of her future. Maud has certainly had more than one attack of depression, one at least being of several years' duration. The concordance in psychosis is very striking in view of the extreme dissimilarity of the environment of the twins. Maud has recovered while Marion has not, but circumstances have been very much more in favour of Maud than her sister. (p. 276)

One sees here the same *complete abandonment of empirical criteria for diagnosis* as we encountered in Kallmann. Moreover, a person's *whole life* is to be categorized as concordant or discordant with another person's *whole life*. How easy it is to pick one episode, or phase, or component, in one person's life and match it for concordance with the whole of another's.

In this way Stephen (215, 211) can be diagnosed as schizophrenic, but hardly on empirical grounds, were this diagnosis not genotypically demanded by the prior diagnosis of his co-twin.

Thus, *Slater uses his assumption of concordance to make his diagnoses concordant, and then uses the count up of his concordant diagnoses to "prove" concordances, and validate his diagnoses.*

The genetic investigation of Kallmann, Slater maintains, "supports the validity of the diagnostic schema" (p. 18). Indeed it does, since, like him, Kallmann finds the concordance figures he himself created.

Slater's suggestion, that errors in diagnosis will tend to cancel out since some schizophrenic psychoses may be affective ones (1953, p. 66), and vice versa, does not hold, because his bias (he is indeed quite open about it) is to diagnose in terms of the "probability" that he presupposes of the genetic hypothesis he purports to be testing. And as we noted above, this bias is so strong that he will even invent a diagnosis in the absence of any empirical evidence whatever (4, 118).

Yet these figures, while they can and will reflect his bias, cannot give him more than he has put into them. Slater's concordances end with his own diagnoses.

Since course, outcome, duration yield no concordances, Slater has recourse to a further example of duplex reasoning. "Environment" is always at hand to explain away dissimilarity, the genes are always at hand to explain similarity. Thus, we are told:

> There is little to be learned from a statistical examination of the duration of the illness of the twins. *There are too many accidental causes of variation in this respect for a comparison to be worthwhile.* (italics mine) (p. 58)

It is very doubtful if mental hospitals are more "dissimilar" than are the multifarious circumstances of the outside world, or that dissimilarity of environmental circumstances generally increases following manifest psychoses.

One doubts if he would suggest that *similarity* of environment was responsible if *concordance* for course and duration of illness had been found. Dissimilar environmental circumstances spring to his mind as a plausible explanation for "discordances," but similarities of environmental conditions do not spring to his mind when he finds concordances.

What Slater has found in fact is that there is concordance for "Slater schizophrenia" but not for clinical schizophrenia. "Thought disorder, therefore, like other deteriorative symptoms [!] shows little sign of being genetically determined" (p. 64).

Slater's "discovery" that "thought disorder," hitherto regarded as one of the cardinal symptoms, is a "deteriorative" symptom is interesting. By another most remarkable sleight of hand he introduces what he calls *positive* moods as signs of schizophrenic illness (depression, periods of elation, agitation or anxiety, or "any marked or rapid change in emotional level"), rather than as positive contraindications. Under "negative" moods he lists apathy, social withdrawal, and inappropriateness or flattening of affect. By this conjuring trick, "moods" that are *positively non*schizophrenic, that are, in the view of many, actual contraindications of schizophrenia, are used to establish concordance for the strange condition of "Slater schizophrenia." In concordant Slater schizophrenics, however, no concordance is found for the "negative moods," which, one recalls, are no less than thought disorder, one of the primary and fundamental symptoms of *clinical* schizophrenia (pp. 58, 59)!

In diagnosing schizophrenia so often without or against empirical evidence, when his presuppositions render it "probable," and in refusing to diagnose it when clinical evidence is available, if his *presuppositions* render it improbable, he cannot stem the inrush of facts at all points at once.

His efforts become almost heroic as they become more frantic. The classical signs of schizophrenia (changes in thought and affect and withdrawal) become deteriorative artifacts: evidence against schizophrenia becomes evidence for it. Phenomenological discordance is seen as genetic concordance. (Affective illnesses occurring in the co-twins of schizophrenics are only apparently, not "basically," affective.) The "diversity of environmental" influences is introduced to account for lack of phenomenological concordance, etc. Finally, where such discordance is too complete to be entirely spirited away, it only "apparently" controverts the genetic hypothesis.

His Alice in Wonderland reason goes like this:

I have here 200 pegs: 100 are round and 100 are square. Each round peg has a number, 1 to 100, and each square peg has a number, 1 to 100.

The 100 round pegs are seen by most people as *red* some of the time.

By the way some of the square pegs have been lost, for instance, No. 57, but we know there once was a square peg of that number.

Now children, we will do a piece of scientific research. The object of this research is to show you that each round peg and each square peg of the same number are the same color, in most cases.

Now let us take round peg No. 1. This is orange, but you can see that it is more red than black, so it is clearly really red. Now we cannot find square peg No. 1, but someone has said that it used to be colored, so it is most probably red. This shows that No. 1 round peg and No. 1 square peg are concordant for red.

Now let us take No. 2 pegs. No. 2 round peg is red as you can see. No. 2 square peg is white, but if we don't lose it, it may turn red, so we had better be safe and call it red. This shows that pegs No. 2 are concordant for red.

No. 3 round peg is interesting. Some people see it red and some see it blue. No. 3 square peg is hardly colored at all (to the untrained eye it even looks colorless), but if you hold it under a strong red light you will see that it is red. Hence pegs No. 3 are concordant.

No. 4 square peg is interesting. One can see that this peg is black. Now if we look carefully we can see that this is because it has been *painted*. If it hadn't been painted black, it would be some other color naturally, and since No. 4 round peg is red, it is clear that No. 4 square peg would much more probably have been red than anything else. Ergo: pegs No. 4 are concordant for red.

Now we see that both No. 5 pegs have been painted many different colors, but you can see that there is some red in them, so they are clearly both basically red pegs.

And so on.

Some aspects of onset, however, are significantly concordant. This "is strong evidence that the type of onset is genetically determined" (1953, p. 59).

As with Kallmann, our main concern has been to focus on the reliability and validity of the *uncorrected* figures.

It is instructive, however, to note briefly Slater's account of his way of arriving at a "reasonable" concordance figure (p. 54) by statistical means, *after* his diagnoses have been made.

> There are in all 41 pairs of uniovular twins of which one member, the propositus, was schizophrenic, and in 28 of these pairs the other member was found to be likewise schizophrenic. Together these two figures give a concordance rate of 68.3 per cent. Such an estimate, however, takes no account of age, and is more inaccurate than it need be. The usual methods of allowing for age are not very satisfactory. It is customary in twin investigations to deal with the partners of the propositi as if they constituted an ordinary sample of the population. Weinberg's shorter method is used, which allocates no risk of schizophrenia to persons under the age of 14, a half-risk between 14 and 40, and a full share of the risk after 40. Using this method we would reduce our total of 41 by half the number of those twins who when last observed were under 40; as 23 twins of our propositi failed to reach this age, the concordance figure would become $^{28}/_{29.5} = 94.9$ per cent. *Such a figure has little meaning.* Alternatively, we might apply the reduction for age only to the partners who never became schizophrenic. *This is logically incorrect,* as Schulz has shown; *but in the present case it leads to a more reasonable concordance figure* of $^{28}/_{37.5} = 74.7$ percent. (italics mine)

Slater's final figure has no other "meaning" or justification than that it looks a likely figure to Slater. He might as well play at bingo as at statistics. The figure of 94.9 percent is arrived at by the same method as Kallmann uses, and if Slater finds little meaning in his own figure of 94.9 percent, presumably he attaches no more to Kallmann's "corrected" figures. The method employed by Kallmann and dropped by Slater is the so-called Weinberg method. "It was devised," according to Planansky (1955), "for estimating risk probability within groups of relatives as they occur in a population sample, but not for estimating manifestation probability within genetically identical pairs" (p. 129).

THE ARGUMENT

Having considered the family, twin family, and twin methods of Kallmann and Slater with particular reference to diagnosis, I now wish to consider some of the more logical arguments put forward in support of the genetic hypothesis collateral with the actual research.

There is a strong tendency for supporters of the genetic hypothesis to befuddle the issue with statements such as the following.

> To those who recognize mental disease as a problem of human biology, genetical inquiries are meaningful and important; to those who are believers in mental processes unassociated with biochemical or structural changes, genetics will appear pointless." (Book, 1960, p. 23)

Lest there be any doubt, I assume for present purposes that no thought, feeling, action occurs unassociated with biochemical or structural changes. I regard genetics as a basic biological discipline.

If we maintain that "schizophrenia" is not a disease or group of diseases, but rather a social event or series of social events, this does not suppose that they occur in some disembodied realm. They occur in the transactions between persons who are physical presences to each other. We shall attempt to show that our theoretical stance enables us to decipher the intelligibility of social events that otherwise, as in the pages of such "geneticists," make no sense. We have tried to show that the figures arrived at by Kallmann and Slater have to be interpreted as the precipitate of their reciprocal interactions with particular others, and that we can render these figures intelligible only by seeing their profoundly subjective nonreciprocal nature, that is, as an expression of a congealed and falsified reciprocity.

The Biological Plausibility of the Genetic Hypothesis

Since Kallmann and Slater like to imply that their theory is firmly founded on biological principles, let us consider this assertion on its own ground.

Slater states the foundations upon which twin work is based as follows.

> . . . being of identical make-up uniovular twins must resemble one another in all particulars in which the genes play a part and must be more alike in these respects than are binovular twins or sibs; any differences between them must be attributable to the environment. *In creating them nature has provided man with the opportunity of observing a controlled experiment.* (1953, p. 6)

I doubt if many biologists would regard the data on twins as affording a controlled experiment, except by way of a very attenuated and imperfect analogy. Various experimental geneticists have made this point, and sounded a note of caution against the too ready acceptance of the genetic hypothesis as "established": e.g. see discussions by Stern (1960), Fuller and Thompson (1960).

It is notable that Slater, despite himself, concedes the main issue.

> The environmental hypothesis, that overt abnormality in the parent has its effect on the child through the environment, cannot be excluded, but it is not plausibly reconciled with the difference between the schizophrenic and the affective groups. (1953, p. 39)

Not only is there no "controlled" experiment of nature in existence in this respect, but the whole definition of "the environment," and the evaluation of its role, is of a most simplistic kind in the work of Kallmann and Slater.

The ability to be mentally adjusted as well as the ability to react to "unadjustable" circumstances with a true psychosis must be regarded as a unique expression of the attainment of human status in the evolutionary development of man's mental equipment and cultural setting. These abilities depend . . . on the common denominator of hereditary potentialities, since it can be shown without difficulty that similar mental reactions of a normal or psychopathological variety are produced by similar environmental circumstances only in a certain number of persons exposed to them. (Kallmann, 1948, p. 251)

He tells us that

. . . certain persons exist, who seem capable of adapting themselves to varying combinations of distressing circumstances without the development of a progressive psychotic process. The list of frustrations, known to produce no severe psychosis in some people, is practically unlimited and extends from physical hardships such as starvation, complete exhaustion, and prolonged malignant disease, to extreme emotional stress, and to a great number of behavioral inadequacies of the parents. (Kallmann, 1952, p. 283)

and asserts that

Beyond doubt, the tendency to deemphasize genetic factors as potential causes of behavior disorders is an occupational hazard of our profession and older than psychiatry itself as a social phenomenon. Whether accomplished by fiat or the Promethean power of allegoric expression, this tendency easily grows into a habit. While it may be obscurable by fluid levels of abstraction, it is sufficiently potent to deflect much investigative and therapeutic effort. Neither conceptually nor for purposes of guidance can the resultant attitude be expected to be of any more help than the affirmation of a fruitless daylight search for owls in Athens or for coal pits in the heart of Newcastle. (Kallmann, 1958, p. 548)

A very good description of Kallmann's and Slater's own work.

Slater states:

In the schizophrenic twins, when the concordant are
compared with the discordant uniovular pairs, there is
no sign of greater similarity in the very early lives of the
former than in those of the latter. A large degree of early
dissimilarity may go with later concordance in respect of
mental disorder.

The pair of twins in whom there was the most striking
degree of early difference is a case in point. These twins,
Lily and Mary, came from a psychiatrically normal family. (1953, p. 45)

It is extremely instructive to examine the texture of the
evidence in yet another crucial case. Here is Slater's presentation of the early lives of this pair whose lives afford
"the most striking degree of early difference" in his whole
study.

History of the twins. Lily weighed 9 lb. at birth, Mary
only 3½ lb. Mary was breast-fed, Lily bottle-fed. Mary
was never as strong as her twin, but neither had any
serious illness. They were not nervous children. Both
went to school from 5 to 14, and left from the top standard; but Lily was more backward while Mary won
prizes and says she had all the brains, "hers as well as
mine." They were not mistaken at school as Lily was
fatter and not clever. They were not at all alike in their
ways; Mary was her dad's girl and took after him, Lily
after her mother; Lily was placid, Mary more fiery. They
grew up rather differently; Lily thought herself a fine
lady and didn't like housework or hard work; Mary enjoyed housework and gave herself no airs. Mary would
mix with anyone, Lily was too much of a madam. Both
were fond of children; Mary liked animals, Lily disliked
them, cats particularly. Lily hated looking after sick people and was not kind to the father, but Mary was of
kinder disposition and looked after him when he was ill.
Lily never liked the cold, Mary didn't mind it. Both were
cheerful but moody, and were rather quiet when
younger. Mary has been much more cheerful since the
change of life. Both preferred men to women friends,
and have had many love affairs. (1953, p. 127)

Is one surprised to note that the sole informants for the above are *Mary* (who won all the prizes, was not so fat, was her daddy's girl, who gave herself no airs—*not* like Lily . . . and was of a kinder disposition, etc.), and a sib four years younger?

However, even if the opposite held, namely, that each environment was similar, it would, according to Kallmann (1958), not weaken the geneticist case.

> The popular notion that the behavior patterns of one-egg twins are alike chiefly because of unusual similarity in their early environments has yet to be substantiated. If confirmed, the argument would only strengthen rather than weaken any correctly formulated genetic theory. Psychodynamic concepts, too, are built on the premise that man is selective in respect to important aspects of his life experiences and so can be thought of as "creating his own environment." (p. 543)

With this two-headed penny it is not clear how Kallmann can lose. A "correctly formulated" genetic theory will be strengthened *whatever* the facts. What now of a "controlled experiment" of nature?

The issue whether concordant twins have similar or dissimilar early "environments" gets dissolved in Kallmann's greed to have his cake and to eat it. The corollary that "it is a well-established" fact that the psychotic twin or other sibling shares the same environment with the "normal" sibling is a spurious one.

In a close study of over twenty-six families we have never found this to be true. The foregoing critique, in our view, establishes the fact that the counter assertions of geneticist researchers on this score cannot be relied upon.

It is as though to say that the two boxers—the winner and the loser—and the referee all shared the same environment because they were all there in the same ring at the one time.

Amazingly enough, until the last fifteen years or so, no studies existed on the different interactions within the families of psychotics. It has now been realized that we also do not know what goes on in "ordinary" families. We each know, from the inside, perhaps only two or three families at most; we each of us have to admit that we know as little about families in our own society, from *within*, as we know about the inside of the earth. Our own present investigation, it is claimed, goes further in the direction of revealing the internal family interactivity in families of psychotics than any other study so far reported. We have also studied by the same method a limited number of "ordinary" families.

We wish to stress that many of the psychotic families presented a perfectly ordinary aspect. The family members are often not plainly abnormal. However, one does not have to dig deep to get at what we believe to be the significant material. But one has to use a special method to bring this surface material to light.

It is not intended here to extend this critique to a review of reviews, but the reader is referred to the critical appraisals of the literature by Planansky (1955), Bleuler (1951), Alanen (1958), and Jackson (1960). These, especially the last three, approach with great reserve the theory that only some people, by virtue of a specific genotype which differentiates them sharply from ordinary people, can be schizophrenic.

Contra Slater, in genetically similar individuals it is not possible to assume that similarity of behavior is genetic, and dissimilarity is environmental. Slater indeed states that only the second of these hypotheses can be "safely" held. Yet he assumes both in practice. In fact, the issue is wrongly posed. By attributing all dissimilarity in uniovular pairs to "environment," he is operating with an unjustifiable cause-effect model. The implication is that given the "same" environment, two genetically identical human individuals would behave identically. This is an unwarranted assumption. The immediate human "environment" consists of a nexus of human agents interacting with the person under given material conditions. This interaction is reciprocal (or dialectical). It seems most likely that the genes provide a range of possibilities, setting the horizons or limits to the actions and reactions that each person has available to him in the interaction situation. "Identical" twins brought up in similar environments are by no means necessarily "identical" in personality variables (Newman *et al.*, 1937).

Slater's statement therefore requires crucial recasting.

Uniovular twins must resemble one another in all particulars which are primarily determined by gene action.

Gene action, on the one hand, and experience and behavior, on the other, are mediated by many intervening media or levels, at each of which interactions and transactions occur, both within the intraorganic environment and between the organism and the extraorganic milieu (Fuller and Thompson, 1960, pp. 341–345).

Such a construct is consistent with the finding of Newman *et al.* (1937) that identical twins correlate most highly on physical characteristics, which seem therefore to be minimally influenced by the extrauterine interpersonal environment. They found, however, that intelligence, educational achievement, personality, and temperament, in that order, appeared less and less *directly* affected by gene action.

It is consistent with the latest research in the genetics of behavior to adopt the following initial provisional assumptions. Genic action is primarily at an enzyme-metabolic-tissue level. As one moves away from the site of primary gene action, it becomes less and less meaningful to suppose that the gene assembly makes identifiably specific contributions, and where we come to the experiential and behavioral levels in human beings, we can no longer employ the same cause-effect model as we can when it is a question of specific physical traits. Furthermore, it is possible to conceive of many different levels of behavior—and it is possible to conceive that gene action determines some "levels" more directly than others, for instance, "instinctive" (i.e. gene-determined) response systems. It is extremely unlikely that all human behavior is entirely a mosaic or chain of directly gene-determined response systems. Genic action in man probably allows on the contrary, a considerable pluripotentiality in experiences and behavior in the one individual.

We would find it conceivable therefore that two identical twins may establish, on the basis of identical genic assemblies, different person-world patterns of interaction, since the genic monitoring of behavior leaves open an as yet undetermined range of indeterminacy.

In identical twins we have before us two historical systems of interaction between two originally identical gene sets and their originally similar environments.

The unattenuated geneticist argument of Kallmann insists on a specific genotype as the necessary though not the sufficient condition for the development of "true" schizophrenia.[5]

While adult experience and behavior is several steps away from primary gene action, genetical diseases can be taken to be, in the present state of knowledge, metabolic defects. No metabolic defects have been found specific to schizophrenia, nor have any been correlated to schizophrenia. Nor, in our view, is any single unit of behavior or experience specific to schizophrenia.

In Kallmann's view, as we saw, there can be no "true" schizophrenia in the absence of this genotype. Only certain people with the schizophrenia genotype are schizophrenic, that is, everyone with this genotype may not be phenotypically schizophrenic, and phenotypical schizophrenics may not be "authentic," that is, genotypic, schizophrenics,

---

[5] Slater is more cautious: "I would not like to exclude the possibility of psychoses of schizophrenic type of purely environmental causation, but would imagine that they are rare. In the majority of schizophrenic psychoses the heredity predisposition has probably played an essential role. Those without this hereditary factor would therefore be practically immune to the disease. . . . Having the predisposition, however, one will not develop the disease unless other factors, environmental and genetical, conspire against one" (1953, p. 49).

He states that he has only one pair in which "there is a marked degree of difference in the psychological situation" (p. 48, i.e. Lily and Mary, see above).

but all "true" schizophrenics will have the specific genotype.

A further difficulty faces the geneticist here.

Neither the "uncorrected" nor any "corrected" figures
fit any genetic theory sufficiently for geneticists to agree on
any interpretation. It is difficult to see how figures that can
be interpreted in totally different genetic terms, from poly-
genes to single dominant or single recessive (dominant
with low penetrance, recessive with high expressivity, with
modifiers perhaps offering "resistance," etc., etc., sex-linked
or not sex-linked), cannot also be interpreted as indicating
no specific genotype at all behind all the smoke.

A typical geneticist argument is given by Book (1960).

> A simple recessive type of inheritance is ruled out by the
> fact that the corrected risk figures for families of actual
> schizophrenics do not differ to a significant degree be-
> tween parents (33), siblings, and children with one or
> no affected parent. Recently Slater has come to the same
> conclusion.
>
> This explanation has to include the assumption of what
> is commonly called a "reduced penetrance," at least in
> the heterozygotes—i.e., the presence of a genetic factor
> that for one reason or another does not actually and visi-
> bly affect the person carrying it. The concept of pene-
> trance in human genetics has often been ridiculed. *It has
> been argued that by applying the proper penetrance a
> reasonable fit can be obtained with an optional Men-
> delian ratio. This is, of course, to a certain extent true, as
> it is also true of any senseless use of a statistical concept
> which was designed to describe a phenomenon but not
> to explain it.* (italics mine) (p. 29)

What an extraordinary last sentence! If it is true "to a
certain extent" or completely, it is certainly no *less* true
because it is also true of other senseless applications of statistical concepts.

It is hardly more satisfactory to state:

> . . . the question of how to designate a mode of trans-
> mission that seems distinguished by a specific unit factor

for the entire syndrome, plus a number of modifying genes responsible for the variable clinical expressions of the main genotype, has become more or less a matter of semantics. (Kallmann, 1958, p. 546)

or that the classification of dominance or recessiveness may now be regarded as no more than "operational definitions for counselling purposes."

The geneticist argument uses various total falsehoods, uncorroborated fantasy, and half-truths as corroborative evidence for the theory.

This is simply to say that given the diagnosis of schizophrenia in a family nexus, in a parent, a sib, a twin, etc., an expectancy figure can be given for particular categories of relatives, and that the explanation of this statistic is entirely speculative. And it has recently become more clear that no organic theory can help out any more at this point. ". . . The primary physiodynamic substrata of a schizophrenic process remains veiled in mystery" (Kallmann, 1958, p. 547).

Kallmann thought, however, that he was on the way to a breakthrough in this area in 1938. One does not wish needlessly to bring out scientific skeletons from the cupboards, but it is worth pondering over some of Kallmann's utterances at that time, both since he still has not repudiated them, and since, still lingering like the grin of the Cheshire cat, they have not yet entirely faded from the scene (e.g. Mayer-Gross, 1954).

This bears on the following.

3. In all the degrees of blood-relationship to our probands, there is a significant agreement between the expectancy figures of schizophrenia and mortality rates of tuberculosis. This concordance reaches so far that in estimating the respective statistics, we find the ratio of proband-siblings to proband-children, and the ratio of grandchildren to children of probands, to be exactly the same for the expectancy of schizophrenia and for the mortality from tuberculosis.

4. This statistical correlation *establishes conclusive*

proof of the direct genetic relationship between predisposition to schizophrenia and heredito-constitutional low resistance to tuberculous infection. It leads to the assumption that these tendencies are gene-coupled, and take the same recessive hereditary course.

5. The question of the anatomical substratum for the positive correlation between the predisposition to schizophrenia and hereditary low resistance to tuberculosis can be answered only tentatively at present. However, there is good reason to believe that the primary and determining hereditary factor for the development of schizophrenia and tuberculosis is based on a certain inherited tissue insufficiency, rather than on a similarity of physical structure or on some toxic-endocrine organic change per se.

6. The most plausible hypothesis at the moment is that a hereditary functional weakness of the reticuloendothelial system (active mesenchyme) is the common heredito-constitutional basis for the tendency to schizophrenia and the susceptibility to tuberculous infection. (italics mine) (Kallmann, 1938, p. 256).

The genetic connection between both disease groups is proven by the consistent increase of the mortality from tuberculosis in all sub-groups of our survey, and particularly by our finding that this death rate is much higher in the descendants of the nuclear group than in those of the peripheral group, and that it is always highest in the categories with the largest figures for the expectancy of schizophrenia. . . . We then discover in all categories of consanguinity such *a startling correspondence between the expectation of schizophrenia and mortality from tuberculosis* that the ratio of frequency between the siblings and children of probands, and again between the grandchildren and children, is exactly the same for the expectancy of schizophrenia and for the mortality from tuberculosis.

This statistical result is so unequivocal that it excludes all possibilities of coincidence, and can only be interpreted as a genuine gene-coupling of the tendency to schizophrenia and the heredito-constitutional susceptibility to tuberculous infection. It also indicates an identical pattern of hereditary transmission for these two predispositions, and confirms the assumption that both schizophrenia and tuberculosis represent recessive traits. (italics mine) (p. 271)

There should be no need to labor this point. All that Kallmann failed to do was to look at families of tubercular patients and see what the morbidity rate for schizophrenia was in them. Moreover, of course, one has yet another demonstration of Kallmann's uncritical dogmatism and lack of scientific caution when schizophrenia is in question. He held at that time (and appears still to hold some attenuated version of this theory) the "heredity-circle" view of schizophrenia.

This truly comic notion is expressive enough of the type of thinking that still characterizes psychiatric biologism. Planansky (1955) characterizes it in these terms:

Luxenburger has pushed the unitary genetic concept to an extreme by recognizing as a true schizoid personality only those cases which occur in a family with a schizophrenic patient. In an endeavor to connect the genetic approach with Kretschmer's constitutional concepts, he built an arbitrary circle of heredity ("Erbkreis") of schizophrenia. Starting from the observation that the schizophrenic family features are distinguished by a definite, though vaguely described coloring through the prevailing body build and temperament, he grants specific genetic significance to any physical or mental aberration which can be somehow linked with schizophrenia. Thus, tuberculosis has its place in the "Erbkreis" because of the alleged close genetic correlation between the susceptibility to tuberculosis and schizophrenia. The common denominator is supposed to be the inability to form adequate connective tissue, and, thus, there is overlapping into the "Erbkreis" of the connective tissue weakness. The latter results from defective mesodermal development, manifested by paucity of pigment and leptosomia. Furthermore, there is overlapping with status dysgraphicus. Apparently, an ideal representant of the "Erbkreis" would be a blond, blue-eyed, tubercular schizophrenic with a concealed spina bifida, and supported by flat feet. (pp. 138–139)

Manfred Bleuler (1955) judiciously summed up the position.

Genetic research has followed an entirely new direction within the past ten years. Mendelian research, in the classical meaning of the term, has almost completely disappeared. We have seen the end of the period of research introduced by Rudin in 1916 in which the chief goal of research in schizophrenia was the strengthening of Kraepelin's system by reducing the latter's disease-units to Mendelian inherited characteristics. Some investigators, to be sure, still mention and discuss simple Mendelian formulae for the hereditary course of the disease called "the" schizophrenia; among these, the simple-recessive type is most frequently named. . . . On the contrary, however, one finds that the great majority of recent works on genetics attacks quite different problems. For one thing, difficulties with family research as such have discouraged people from looking for simple Mendelian principles of hereditary transmission: *the resulting figures on hereditary disorders within a family could easily and with mathematical precision be brought into accord with the most diverse formulae for heredity;* yet, whenever new facts became known, they failed to fit any one formula offered. Furthermore, it turned out that the figures on hereditary taint do not reveal static biological values, but vary to a great extent with the formulations of different schools. On the other hand, the development of the general doctrine of schizophrenia tends to break away from the old Mendelian ideas about genetic research. Less and less support is being given to the viewpoint that schizophrenia is a biological and etiological entity; more and more, we discover, in the individual patient, that the individual genesis of the disease is to be found in the effect of a unique environment on a unique *Anlage.* Also the increasing importance of the concept of *Gestalt* and of totality in psychopathology diminishes the significance of the classical Mendelian theory. Genetics in psychiatry is dominated by the concept of a reciprocal action between totality and the individual; Mendelianism in its old form only understands the individual as separate from the totality. (1951, pp. 10–11)

No further evidence has come to light since then to belie this statement.

There occur, however, even in the *corrected* figures of Kallmann and Slater, but particularly in a study by Penrose (1945) (left fascinatingly alone by the geneticists), a number of purely statistical correlations that ill fit any genetic theory. They are all predictable, however, in terms of a correctly stated sociogenic theory.

Our own position, therefore, is in no way to deny the basic principles of human genetics. It is just in terms of these basic principles themselves that we cannot accept the specific genotype theory of schizophrenia, even in the slightly attenuated form held by Slater.

On the other hand, the theory we have ourselves propounded is consistent with the existence of such figures as the geneticists have produced, if their manner of production is properly understood.

I shall simply list some of these predictable expectancies without discussion of their significance, which can most appropriately be undertaken in the course of the evaluation of our own data.

1. The child is rather more likely to be schizophrenic if the mother is schizophrenic than if the father is schizophrenic.

2. The concordance for schizophrenia in siblings will be rather higher than between parents and children because parents do not share their own first fifteen years with their children.

3. One expects mother-daughter, mother-son pairs to occur more frequently than father-son, father-daughter pairs.

4. One expects that there will be more sister-sister than

NONGENETIC CONCORDANCES

Same Sexed DZ Twins:

Lange: Criminality   MZ 66 DZ 54 (same sex) 14 (opposite sex)

Rosanoff: Schizophrenia   MZ 86 DZ 56 (same sex) 21 (opposite sex)

Slater: 9 out of 11 female   DZ, 2 male (only possible schizophrenics)

Essen-Moller: of 5 concordant   DZ, 4 are F

Kallmann   85.6 17.6 (same sex; female-male not given)

                                    To 11.5 opposite sex

Family Groupings:

Zehnder: 84% of pairs were female   Sisters (11F to 2M within 5 years)

                                                     (14F to 2M within 10 years)

Penrose: *Pairs of relatives, frequency:*   *Of total samples:*

                  Sister-Sister   8.7% Fathers

                  Brother-Brother   24.5% Mothers

                  Mother-Daughter   30.0% Relatives

Folie à deux: Sisters—4.5 to 1 over other relatives

               Mother-Daughter—16 times greater than Father-Daughter

               Mother-Son—8 times greater than Father-Son

(*Jackson, 1960, p. 65*)

brother-sister pairs, and perhaps more, certainly not fewer, sister-sister than brother-brother pairs.

5. Dizygotic twins, *especially sister-sister*, will have significantly higher concordance than ordinary brother-sister pairs: their concordance will be perhaps significantly higher, and certainly not lower, than ordinary sister-sister pairs.

Penrose's study has the merit of simply taking diagnoses as he finds them: but to make sense of his figures he has had to suggest a sex-linkage theory for the genetic transmission of schizophrenia—a suggestion that will require some readjustments of diagnoses in its light before figures of other geneticists could begin to support it. He had, however, to take on trust ordinary psychiatric diagnosis. Studies of the reliability of such diagnoses (Kreitman, 1961) are not encouraging.

The work of Kallmann and Slater has been examined with particular reference to the validity of their diagnosis of schizophrenia. The conclusion and the moral are the same: You cannot make a statistical silk purse out of a clinical sow's ear.

REFERENCES

Alanen, Y. O. (1958). "The Mothers of Schizophrenic Patients." *Acta Psychiat. et Neurol. Scandinav.* Supplement *124*:33.

Bleuler, M. (1955). "Research and Changes in Concepts in the Study of Schizophrenia, 1941–1950." In Babcock, H. H., ed., *Bulletin of the Isaac Ray Medical Library*, 3 (January–April 1955). Reprinted from: (1951). *Fortschritte der Neurologie, Psychiatrie und ihrer Grenzegebiete*, 19:9/10. Stuttgart: Georg Thieme Verlag.

Book, J. A. (1960). "Genetical Aspects of Schizophrenic Psychoses." In Jackson, D. D., ed., *The Etiology of Schizophrenia*. New York: Basic Books.

Craike, W. H., and Slater, E. (1945). "Folie à Deux in Uniovular Twins Reared Apart." *Brain*, 68:213–221.

Fuller, J. L., and Thompson, W. R. (1960). *Behavior Genetics.* New York: Wiley.

Jackson, D. D. (1960). "A Critique of the Literature of the Genetics of Schizophrenia." In Jackson, D. D., ed., *The Etiology of Schizophrenia.* New York: Basic Books.

Kallmann, F. J. (1938). *The Genetics of Schizophrenia.* New York: J. J. Augustin.

———. (1946). "The Genetic Theory of Schizophrenia." *Amer. J. Psychiat., 103*:309–322.

———, and Mickey, J. S. (1946). "The Concept of Induced Insanity in Family Units." *J. Nerv. Ment. Dis., 104* (September 1946).

———. (1948). "Genetics in Relation to Mental Disorders." *J. Ment. Sci., 94*:250–257.

———. (1950). "The Genetics of Psychoses: Analysis of 1,232 Twin Index Families." *Congrés International de Psychiatrie, Paris, 6*:1–40.

———. (1952). "Genetic Aspects of Psychoses." In *The Biology of Mental Health and Disease.* New York: Paul B. Hoeber, Inc. (medical div. of Harper & Brothers), for the Milbank Memorial Fund.

———. (1953). *Heredity in Health and Mental Disorder.* London: Chapman & Hall.

———. (1956). "The Genetics of Human Behavior." *Amer. J. Psychiat., 113*:496–501.

———. (1958). "The Use of Genetics in Psychiatry." *J. Ment. Sci., 104*:542–552 (April 1958).

Kreitman, N. (1961). "The Reliability of Psychiatric Diagnosis." *J. Ment. Sci., 107*:876–887.

Mayer-Gross, W., Slater, E., and Roth, M. (1954). *Clinical Psychiatry.* London: Cassell & Co., Ltd.

Newman, H. H., Freeman, F. N., and Holzinger, K. J. (1937). *Twins: A Study of Heredity and Environment.* Chicago: University of Chicago Press.

Penrose L. S. (1945). *Survey of Cases of Familial Mental Illness.* Roneo. Summarized in: (1945). "Survey of Cases of Familial Mental Illness." *Digest Neurol. and Psychiat., 13*: 644.

Planansky, K. (1955). "Heredity in Schizophrenia." *J. Nerv. Ment. Dis., 122*:121–142.

Rosenthal, D. (1959). "Schizophrenia in Monozygotic Twins." *J. Nerv. Ment. Dis.*, 129:1–10.

———. (1961). "Sex Distribution and the Severity of Illness Among Samples of Schizophrenic Twins." *J. Psychiat. Research.*, 1:26–37.

Slater, E. (1953). "Psychotic and Neurotic Illnesses in Twins." *Medical Research Council, Special Report No. 278.* London: H.M. Stationery Office.

Stern, C. (1960). *Principles of Human Genetics.* San Francisco and London: W. H. Freeman & Co.

APPENDIX B

PHILADELPHIA ASSOCIATION, 1964–1974

Excerpts from a recent brochure of the Philadelphia Association, of which Dr. Laing is chairman, describe some of the aims and accomplishments of the group.

> Philadelphia (Greek): brotherly or sisterly love. ". . . I have set before thee an open door, and no man can shut it." Revelation 3:8

Extracts from Articles of Association

To relieve mental illness of all descriptions, in particular schizophrenia.

To undertake, and further, research into the causes of mental illness, the means of its detection and prevention, and its treatment.

To provide, and further, the provision of residential accommodation for persons suffering or who have suffered from mental illness.

To provide financial assistance for poor patients.

To promote and organise training in the treatment of schizophrenia and other forms of mental illness.

To hold seminars, conferences, and summer schools.

To publish and subsidise publications having any relevance to the objects of the Association.

Our Articles of Association state our purposes in terms appropriate to our existence as a Charity.

We aim to change the way the "facts" of "mental health" and "mental illness" are seen by many people.

This is more than a new hypothesis inserted into an existing field of research and therapy; it is a proposal to change our whole way of seeing the issues.

Communities

There are seven community households in London. Their accommodation varies from seven to eleven rooms.

One house is owned by one of our members.

One house is held in Trust for the Association by a member.

Two houses are rented on a short-term lease, and are due shortly for demolition.

Two houses are rented on a three-year lease.

One house is rented on a long-term lease.

Each of the houses has a garden; one has a pottery and glasshouse.

It is our concern that these households be asylums, sanctuaries, and places of hospitality.

For those who live there, whatever their roles, these dwellings are crucibles where preconceptions are melted down in the direct experience of the wear and tear, agony and joy, excitement and boredom, hope and despair, of living together.

Training

Our lectures, seminars, study-groups, and workshops are a forum wherein members, associates, students, friends, and visitors share their understanding of the world.

The path followed is a phenomenological one, based on what we learn from a critique of our experience. Specific subjects studied include psychoanalysis, anthropology, phenomenology, music, literature, and different forms of physical and mental training, e.g. Hatha Yoga, aikido . . . seeking, perhaps through indirection, to come to ourselves.

From June 1965 to September 1974, 316 people, 197 men and 119 women, have stayed in our households; of the

316, 142, 80 men and 62 women, had been psychiatric inpatients; of the 316, 288, 182 men and 108 women, have left.

The usual length of stay has been between three months and one year; of the 288 who left, 29, all of whom had been psychiatric inpatients, 9 men and 20 women, have been back in hospital once, or more, since leaving, as far as we know.

REFERENCES

Adler, A. *Practice and Theory of Individual Psychology.* New York: Harcourt, Brace and World, 1927.

Bateson, G., Jackson, D., Haley, J., and Weakland, J. "Toward a Theory of Schizophrenia." *Behavioral Science, 1* (1956), 251–64.

————. *Steps to an Ecology of Mind.* New York: Ballantine Books, 1972.

Bion, W. R. *Experiences in Groups and Other Papers.* New York: Basic Books, 1961.

————. *Learning from Experience.* New York: Basic Books, 1963.

————. *Attention and Interpretation: a Scientific Approach to Insight in Psychoanalysis and Groups.* London: Tavistock Publications, 1970.

Bleuler, M. *Textbook of Psychiatry.* A. A. Brill (Ed.) New York: Dover Books, 1951.

Brodine, V., and Selden, M., eds. *Open Secret: The Kissinger-Nixon Doctrine in Asia.* New York: Harper & Row, 1972.

Chomsky, N. *Syntactic Structures.* The Hague: Mouton, 1957.

————. *Language and Mind.* New York: Harcourt Brace Jovanovich, 1968.

Cohn, N. *The Pursuit of the Millennium.* London: Oxford University Press, 1970.

Evans, R. I. *Conversations with Carl Jung and Reactions from Ernest Jones.* New York: D. Van Nostrand Company, Inc., 1964.

————. *Dialogue with Erich Fromm.* New York: Harper & Row, 1966.

————. *B. F. Skinner: The Man and His Ideas.* New York: E. P. Dutton & Co., Inc., 1968.

————. *Dialogue with Erik Erikson.* New York: E. P. Dutton & Co., Inc., 1969a.

————. *Psychology and Arthur Miller.* New York: E. P. Dutton & Co., Inc., 1969b.

————. "Contributions to the History of Psychology: X Filmed

Dialogues with Notable Contributors to Psychology." *Psychological Reports*, 1969c, 25, 159–164.

————. *Gordon Allport: The Man and His Ideas*. New York: E. P. Dutton & Co., Inc., 1971.

————. *Jean Piaget: The Man and His Ideas*. New York: E. P. Dutton & Co., Inc., 1973.

————. *Carl Rogers: The Man and His Ideas*. New York: E. P. Dutton & Co., Inc., 1975a.

————. *Konrad Lorenz: The Man and His Ideas*. New York: Harcourt Brace Jovanovich, 1975b.

————. *Jung on Elementary Psychology: A Discussion Between Carl Jung and Richard Evans*. New York: E. P. Dutton & Co., Inc., forthcoming.

Freud, S. *The Standard Edition of the Complete Psychological Works of Sigmund Freud*. Edited by J. Strachey. London: Hogarth Press, 1953–

Goffman, E. *The Presentation of Self in Everyday Life*. Garden City, N.Y.: Doubleday Anchor Books, 1959.

Heath, R. G. A Biochemical Hypothesis on the Etiology of Schizophrenia. In Jackson, D. D., ed. *The Etiology of Schizophrenia*. New York: Basic Books, 1960.

————, Martens, S., Leach, B. E., Cohen, M., and Angel, C. "Effects on Behavior in Humans with the Administration of Taraxein." *American Journal of Psychiatry*, 114 (1957), 14–24.

————, Martens, S., Leach, B. E., Cohen, M., and Feigley, C. A. "Behavioral Changes in Nonpsychotic Volunteers Following the Administration of Taraxein, the Substance Obtained from the Serum of Schizophrenic Patients." *American Journal of Psychiatry*, 114 (1958), 917–920.

————, Krupp, I. M., Byers, L. W., and Liljukvist, J. I. "Schizophrenia as an Immunologic Disorder." *Archives of General Psychiatry*, 16(1) (1967), 1–33.

Heidegger, M. *An Introduction to Metaphysics*. Translated by Ralph Manheim. New Haven, Conn.: Yale University Press, 1959.

————. *Being and Time*. New York: Harper & Row, 1962.

Horney, K. *The Neurotic Personality of Our Time*. New York: W. W. Norton, 1937.

————. *Our Inner Conflicts*. New York: W. W. Norton, 1945.

Husserl, E. *Ideas: General Introduction to Pure Phenomenology.* Translated by W. R. Boyce Gibson. New York: The Macmillan Company, 1952.

——. *The Crisis of European Sciences and Transcendental Phenomenology: an Introduction to Phenomenological Philosophy.* Translated and with an introduction by David Carr. Evanston, Ill.: Northwestern University Press, 1970.

Illich, Ivan D. *Medical Nemesis.* London: Calder and Boyars, 1975.

Janov, A. *The Primal Scream: Primal Therapy: The Cure for Neurosis.* New York: Dell Publishing Company, Inc., 1970.

Kallmann, F. J. *Heredity in Health and Mental Disorder.* New York: W. W. Norton, 1953.

——. "The Use of Genetics in Psychiatry." *Journal of Mental Science,* 104 (1958), 542–549.

Kardiner, A. *The Individual and His Society.* New York: Columbia University Press, 1939.

Kraepelin, E. *Lehrbuch der Psychiatrie.* 1883.

Laing, R. D. *The Divided Self; a Study of Sanity and Madness.* London: Tavistock Publications, 1960.

——, and Cooper, D. G. *Reason and Violence; a Decade of Sartre's Philosophy, 1950–1960.* With a foreword by Jean-Paul Sartre. New York: Humanities Press, 1964.

——, Phillipson, H., and Lee, A. R. *Interpersonal Perception: a Theory and a Method of Research.* London: Tavistock Publications, 1966.

——. *The Politics of Experience.* New York: Pantheon Books, 1967.

——. *Self and Others.* 2d rev. ed. New York: Pantheon Books, 1970a.

——. *Knots.* 1st American ed. New York: Pantheon Books, 1970b.

——. *The Politics of the Family, and Other Essays.* 1st American ed. New York: Pantheon Books, 1971.

——, and Esterson, J. A. *Sanity, Madness and the Family: Families of Schizophrenics.* 2d American ed. New York: Basic Books, 1971.

——. *Why Did the Peacock Scream?* New York: Pantheon Books, forthcoming.

Lévi-Strauss, C. *The Savage Mind.* Chicago: The University of Chicago Press, 1966.

Luce, G. *Body Time: Physiological Rhythms in Social Stress.* New York: Pantheon Books, 1971.

Sullivan, H. S. *The Interpersonal Theory of Psychiatry.* Edited by H. S. Perry and M. L. Gawel. New York: W. W. Norton, 1953.

INDEX

INDEX

ABOUT THE AUTHOR

RICHARD I. EVANS received his Ph.D. from Michigan State University and is currently professor of psychology at the University of Houston. He is the Director of the Social Psychology/Behavioral Medicine Research and Graduate Training Group.

A National Science Foundation grant has enabled him to film discussions and complete books with some of the world's foremost behavioral scientists including the distinguished participants in the dialogues in this Praeger Series.

He is a pioneer in public television and in the social psychology of communication, and has published over a hundred articles in the area of social psychology. In addition to the volumes in this Dialogue Series, his books include *Social Psychology in Life* (with Richard Rozelle), *Resistance in Innovation in Higher Education, The Making of Psychology,* and *The Making of Social Psychology.*

His recent honors include the American Psychological Foundation Media Awards for the book, *Gordon Allport: The Man and His Ideas* and the film, "A Psychology of Creativity." He and his colleagues received American Psychological Association Division 13 Research Excellence Awards in 1970, 1973, and 1977 for their work in social psychology in behavioral medicine. He received the Phi Kappa Phi National Distinguished Scholar Award for the 1974-77 Triennium, and the 1980 Ester Farfel Award, the University of Houston's highest award for excellence in teaching, research and service.